New Ideas

by **Larry Evans**

International Grandmaster
U.S. Champion
Three times U.S. "Open" Champion
Canadian "Open" Champion

CORNERSTONE LIBRARY

NEW YORK

Reprinted 1972

This new Cornerstone Library edition is published by arrangement with Pitman Publishing Corp., and is a new revised reprint of the original hardcover edition.

To Ann

Here is a book for you to
learn from when I'm not
there to lose my temper.

CORNERSTONE LIBRARY PUBLICATIONS
Are Distributed By
Simon & Schuster, Inc.
630 Fifth Avenue
New York, New York 10020

Manufactured in the United States of America
under the supervision of
Rolls Offset Printing Co., Inc., N.Y.

Foreword

THE keynote of chemistry is that elements may combine to create new entities. The chessmaster is the chemist of a dimension that is geometrically bounded by 8 × 8. The elements with which he works are *Pawn Structure, Space, Force,* and *Time.* The amateur is vaguely aware that these exist, but he does not know how they interact. He has never learned to manipulate them properly. Masters have been of little help, for they are notoriously inarticulate when it comes to explaining their own thought processes.

My problem has been to translate into principles the habits which are inbred in the master; then to break these down into words. (Here I must own a debt to Ralph Berton, a rabid woodpusher, whose persistent questioning generated greater clarity.) These principles, moreover, are so absolute that if chess is played a thousand years from now they will still be in force. I arrived at them by replaying all my tournament games, analyzing why I either won or lost, and then extracting the quintessence from each one. What is "new" about this book is its formulation. Because it is basic, it is revolutionary.

A famous principle of conservation in physics states that matter may be converted into energy and vice versa, but the total quantity of both together, in a closed system, remains unchanged. The chessboard is a closed system. Our "new ideas" would lead us to suspect that an advantage in any one element may never be lost (assuming "perfect" play thereafter), though it may be converted into other element(s) under the proper conditions. In general, *the whole process of chess technique aims at converting the less durable into the more durable advantage.* What is meant by an "advantage," and how to recognize it, is the domain of this book. The purely tactical problem of how to exploit an advantage is dealt with at length under the illustrative examples, all taken from actual play.

Lately there has been a spate of works on how to win in the opening, how to win in the middle game, how to win in the ending. But a game of chess is an organic whole—there are no miracles—a good position is good, a bad position is bad. So far as I know the only way to win is to outplay your opponent. This book is designed to help you do just that.

Contents

FOREWORD   iii

CHESSBOARD NOTATION   vii

Chapter One

THE EVOLUTION OF CHESS   1

Chess up to the Time of Morphy 1
Paul Morphy and the Romantics: Open Game . . . 4
Wilhelm Steinitz and the Classicists: Closed Game . . 9
Réti and the Hypermoderns: Flank Game . . . 12
The Technicians: Neo-Classical School 15
The Eclectics 17

Chapter Two

PAWN STRUCTURE   22

The Outside Passed Pawn 22
Pawn Structure Determines Strategy 24
Pawn Mobility 25
Passed Pawns 32
Connected, Isolated and Backward Pawns 36
Doubled and Tripled Pawns 46
Weak Squares 52
Pawn Chains 60
The Bad Bishop 67
The Queen Side Majority 68

Chapter Three

FORCE   73

Table of Relative Values 73
The General Pattern for Converting Force into Victory . 75
The Two Bishops 75
The Positional Sacrifice 88
The Temporary Sacrifice 90

Chapter Four

SPACE   96
The Center 96
Mobility 97
Control of Unoccupied Squares 97
A Typical Space Advantage 97
How to Count Space 98
Stability 98
How to Test Stability 99

Chapter Five

TIME   123
Gambits 124
Pins 141

Chapter Six

QUIZ   146
Caution 146
Problems 147
Solutions 153

Chapter Seven

NEW APPROACH TO THE OPENINGS   162
Evaluation 162
Is the First Move an Advantage? 165
Master Practice 166
The Failure of Traditional Evaluation . . . 166
A Self-Contained Evaluation 170
The First Move 171
Reverse Openings 172
The Theory of Symmetrical Positions . . . 175

Chapter Eight

SUMMING UP   179
The Stable Elements 179
The Unstable Elements 180

BIBLIOGRAPHY   182

INDEX OF OPPONENTS   183

The life, the fortune, and the happiness of every one of us and, more or less, of those who are connected with us, do depend on our knowing the rules of a game infinitely more complicated than chess. . . . The chessboard is the world, the pieces are the phenomena of the universe, the rules of the game are what we call the laws of nature. The player on the other side is hidden from us. We know that his play is always fair, just and patient. But we also know, to our cost, that he never overlooks a mistake or makes the slightest allowance for ignorance. To the man who plays well the highest stakes are paid, with that sort of overflowing generosity with which the strong show delight in strength. And one who plays ill is checkmated without hate, but without remorse.

Thomas Henry Huxley, 1887

Chessboard Notation

THIS is a book for advanced beginners and serious students. This explanation is for those who play chess for enjoyment and wish to improve, but have been scared away from chess literature by the cryptic symbols employed.

Chess notation is merely a shorthand for recording the moves of a game so that it may be replayed at some future time. Other than serving as the medium for transmitting these moves to you, these abbreviations have no special significance.

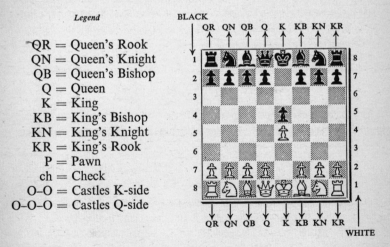

Legend

QR = Queen's Rook
QN = Queen's Knight
QB = Queen's Bishop
Q = Queen
K = King
KB = King's Bishop
KN = King's Knight
KR = King's Rook
P = Pawn
ch = Check
O–O = Castles K-side
O–O–O = Castles Q-side

This position is diagrammed after the opening move **1 P–K4** and Black's reply **1 . . . P–K4**. Note that White's K4 is Black's K5, and vice versa. The hyphen is read as "to." Thus P–K4 is read "Pawn to King Four." In playing over the illustrations in this book you will probably find it helpful to reproduce the diagrammed positions on a board. Follow the analysis on it. If you can follow the variations "blindfolded," i.e., directly from the diagram, so much the better.

CHAPTER ONE: The Evolution of Chess

Chess up to the Time of Morphy

Modern chess, in its infancy, abounded in swashbuckling combinations and brilliancies. Whatever its players may have lacked, it was not imagination. The odd thing was that the leading masters rarely were the victims of their own tactics. The majority of the eighty-five games of the six LaBourdonnais-MacDonnell matches in 1834 were not noted for their brevity. Apparently, lesser mortals never thought to ask why the masters polished off their amateur opposition in short, sparkling "parties," while their own games with each other often were of inordinate length. Masters were possessed of a chess "daemon"—that was all there was to it. They certainly were the last to disturb this common illusion. Their knowledge was guarded jealously, or imparted in private lessons for fancy fees.

What set the masters apart was their grasp of "general principles." The value of Time and the importance of Force had always been recognized—though there were those who argued that odds of Pawn and move are an advantage because they permit Black to develop a rapid attack along the open KB file!

The essential difference between the nineteenth-century outlook and that of the twentieth is that the modern master, when confronted with a choice between a relatively transitory advantage in Time and a rather more permanent one in Space, will generally choose Space. Having confidence in his defensive technique, he will usually submit to a short-term evil for a long-term good. Often this means accepting a difficult though tenable position in exchange for a won endgame, if and when it can be reached.

The early nineteenth-century players did not have very deep insight into the real value of Time. The same piece might be moved five times in the opening, neglecting the harmonious development of the other pieces. Premature attacks were the rule. But the art of defense was in such a relatively backward state that these inferior tactics prevailed. It was not that these players were obtuse—the leading masters of that era would probably excel today—but, like the electric light, the basic principles of chess strategy simply hadn't been invented. Don't think that the pioneers of modern chess were not sharply rebuked with "taking the fun out of the game!" The romantics were so enraptured with aesthetics that they felt cheated when good defense frustrated a brilliancy. They seemed oblivious to the satisfaction that might be derived from a finely played lost game rather than from any number of wins derived through errors of an opponent. At that time a man would probably have been thought mad saying as Napier did after he had lost to Lasker at Cambridge Springs in 1904, "This is the finest game I ever played!" Games in which stodgy defense prevailed were seemingly devoid of beauty—for what beauty was there in grubby, materialistic, defensive strategy? If that was all there was to chess, as well take up whist. The old-timers wanted to witness games worthy of being showered with pieces of gold. They did not realize that if the standard of defense were raised it would inevitably raise the standard of attack.

Many of the so-called "immortal games" strike us today as downright ugly. We lose patience with the defender, who forages with his Queen for material gain while neglecting the development of his minor pieces. Any modern duffer could put up a better defense than the loser. Again, this is not meant to disparage the players of a bygone era—or to minimize the beauty of their conceptions (some of which have never been excelled)—but solely to emphasize how much strategy has progressed since then.

Let us consider two celebrated examples—"The Immortal Game" and "The Evergreen Partie." As with chess "problems," we had better not ask just how the players got into such curious predicaments. But if we omit the preceding moves and simply diagram each position just before the final combination, it then becomes a thing of beauty and a joy to behold! Needless to add, the brilliancy is often superfluous. In Diagram 1, for instance, the prosaic 22 QxP would win just as handily as the text.

Diagram 1

Diagram 2

White to play and win

21	NxPch	K–Q1
22	Q–B6ch!	NxQ
23	B–K7 mate	

White to play and win

21	QxPch!!	KxQ
22	B–B5 dbl. dis. ch! . . .	

Black's replies are all forced.

22	. . .	K–K1
23	B–Q7ch	K–Q1
24	BxN mate	

It is true that there are certain important differences between these two positions. However, the similarities are even more meaningful. In both, Black had moved his Queen many times before the diagrammed position was reached. Both games are still relatively in the opening stage and in both Black is overwhelmingly ahead in material. The major generic difference is that in Diagram 1 Black's pieces are undeveloped (on their original squares), whereas in Diagram 2 Black has mobilized a formidable counterattack and actually threatens mate in one.

This spiritual similarity is no accident—nor is it an accident that Anderssen, who was by far the best of the pre-Morphyites, was on the winning White side in each case.

Along came Morphy, who toyed with Anderssen just as Anderssen had toyed with his contemporaries. After their match in 1858, during which he was decisively trounced, Anderssen wrote: "He who plays Morphy must abandon all hope of catching him in a trap, no matter how cunningly laid, but must assume that it is so clear to Morphy that there can be no question of a false step."

Even this magnanimous tribute fails to credit Morphy's revolutionary new principles—Anderssen himself did not fully appreciate why he had lost! It is noteworthy that Anderssen displays a certain psychological uneasiness in terming his own attacks "traps" and nothing more. Morphy's attacks, on the other hand, always flowed out of the position, organically. Anderssen's were more often an inspiration of the moment. Morphy knew not only how to attack, but also when—and that is why he won.

Morphy defeated all his opponents in similar fashion, then sought for many years to arrange a match with Staunton, the self-proclaimed champion of the world, but in vain.*

In an era when the dynamic young United States was suffering from a cultural inferiority complex, Morphy became a sort of national super-ego. He was hailed by the press as the first American representative to triumph directly over Old World culture. Europeans, loathe to admit that an outlander might possess a talisman unknown to them, first awakened to the fact that maybe their masters had no "daemon" at all. Maybe there were certain principles which, once grasped, would enable anyone to rise in chess as far as his ability admitted. The Royal Game became a little less royal. It became democratic.

Paul Morphy and the Romantics: Open Game

In the late eighteenth century André Philidor, a distinguished composer as well as a good chessplayer (who, by the way, is mentioned in Rousseau's *Confessions*), enunciated his great doctrine that "the Pawn is the soul of chess." This implied that Pawn Structure, being the most inert element, largely determines the character of the position and also the plan appropriate to it (see Diagram 16). In his games, more than his writings, Philidor showed how to assault an enemy fortress by using Pawns as battering rams backed up by heavy pieces.

* For the psychological-minded, we recommend "The Problem of Paul Morphy" by Dr. Ernest Jones, which may be found in that excellent anthology *The Chess Reader* (Greenberg Publishers. New York, *1949*.)

4

Diagram 3

Black's Pawns are battering rams. *Notice how Black has massed both Rooks behind his Pawns. White's apparently impregnable King position has a weakness on KN3. It requires but a few thrusts to demolish it entirely—against bad defense.*

| 1 . . . | P–R5 |
| 2 Q–KB2? | . . . |

Correct is 2 P–KB4! PxBP; 3 N–N4! And white snatches the initiative!

2 . . .	B–B2
3 N–K2	RPxP
4 QxP	QxQch
5 NxQ	N–B5ch
6 K–R1	RxP

Despite the exchange of Queens, Black's attack rages unabated!

7 R–KN1	RxNch
8 KxR	R–R1ch
9 N–R5	RxNch
10 K–N3	N–R6 dis. ch
11 K–N4	R–R5 mate

This patient, closed game did not suit the temperament of Philidor's compatriot, LaBourdonnais, who perceived that this slow, systematic massing of Pawns was inapplicable to the opening. Instead, LaBourdonnais applied to his games the principle of straightforward development in the center. He combatted every developed enemy unit with a force at least equal to it. He pursued the enemy with hand-to-hand fighting, rebuffed him in the center, then sought to establish an advanced central outpost of his own.

Diagram 4

White moves. *Clearly, the struggle here is for control of the center. White has an isolated QP. Black maintains a stout blockade on Q4. It is necessary for White to act quickly, to develop some middle game threats, before Black succeeds in consolidating and reaching an ending where the Pawn Structure will favor him.*

1 P–QR4   . . .

The modern master would probably play N–K5 immediately. LaBourdonnais reasons that you have to give up something to get something. The text weakens White's QN4 square, yet it has an indirect bearing on the center inasmuch as the threat of P–R5 would force Black to relinquish one of the defenders of his Q4 blockade.

1 . . .   **P–QR4**

On 1 . . . NxB; 2 PxN, N–Q4 White may elect the simple 3 Q–Q2, or the sharp 3 BxN, PxB; 4 Q–N3, B–K3; 5 QxNP, R–N1; 6 QxRP, emerging a Pawn ahead after 6 . . . RxP.

2 N–K5   . . .

White uses his QP as a pivot in maintaining an advanced central outpost.

2 . . .   **B–K3**

3 B–B2   . . .

Setting his sights for the K-side

3 . . .   **P–KB4?**

This closes the line of White's K-Bishop, but creates a gruesome weakness on K3, and forever removes the possibility of P–B3, driving the Knight from K5. 3 . . . B–QN5, putting pressure on White's center, and occupying the "hole" on QN5, is a reasonable alternative.

4 Q–K2   . . .

LaBourdonnais develops his Queen with a view to exerting more pressure on the center, via the K-file.

4 . . .   **P–B5**

This opens the line for the K-Bishop, which is serious. Black's lack of strategy is obvious. He should be defending instead of attacking!

5 B–Q2   **Q–K1**

6 QR–K1   **. . .**

Another strong developing move, which exerts still more pressure in the center.

6 . . .   **B–B2**

7 Q–K4   **. . .**

White has completed his build-up. The threat of mate wins material.

7 . . .   **P–N3**

8 BxP   **NxB**

9 QxN   **B–B5**

10 Q–R6   **BxR**

11 BxP!   **PxB**

12 NxNP   **. . .**

White has a winning attack. The remaining moves were: **12 . . . N–B1; 13 Q–R8ch, K–B2; 14 Q–R7ch, K–B3; 15 N–B4, B–Q6; 16 R–K6ch, K–N4; 17 Q–R6ch, K–B4; 18 R–K5 mate.**

After LaBourdonnais' death a dreary period of dry chess, without power or imagination, overtook the chess world. It was Paul Morphy (1837–1884) who revitalized the Romantic tradition. Morphy never massed Pawns in the opening as Philidor had taught. Instead he pushed only one or two Pawns in order to free his pieces and open lines for them, even if it was necessary to sacrifice a Pawn or two in the process. Morphy recognized that Time was more important than Force *in the opening*. His pieces invaded quickly in the center, leaving his harassed opponent no time for methodical Pawn maneuvers. Morphy combined with his flair for the open game a flexibility which so irked his critics that they levelled the accusation which has since been levelled at practically every other great master (particularly Capablanca): the inclination to exchange Queens in order to win a paltry Pawn and nurse it through to victory in the endgame.

These were the characteristics of the open game at which Morphy excelled: some of the center Pawns have been exchanged, the pieces command open lines, a central file has generally been ripped open.

The openings arising from 1 P–K4 are more likely to lead to open positions than 1 P–Q4 because it is easier to force P–Q4 (after 1 P–K4) than it is to force P–K4 (after 1 P–Q4). The reason for this is that Q4 is originally protected whereas K4 is not. QP games generally lead to closed positions, while their KP counterparts lead to more lively play. The tendency of modern chess is away from open games, partly because they have been so extensively analyzed.

Morphy was the first player who fully realized the importance of development. He expressed this in the simple phrase, "Help your pieces so that they can help you." He was often aided by the unnecessarily timid defensive moves of his opponents, or even by their unnecessarily aggressive moves as we have seen in the previous example when Black played 4 . . . P–B5.

MORPHY—AMATEUR, NEW ORLEANS, 1858

Diagram 5

Black moves. *In this position Black is two Pawns ahead, and it is probable that he can win with proper defense. However, he fails to understand the position. He should strive to keep the lines closed, for instance by playing P–KB3 and retreating the Knight to N3 (after White's inevitable P–B4), so as to observe the key square, White's K5. White must be prevented at all costs from opening lines by P–B4 and P–K5. Instead, with his next move, Black solves the problem Morphy has thus far been unable to solve—namely, how to open up diagonals for his two Bishops.*

15 . . .   P–KB4?

A very instructive error. This move opens (1) the K-file, (2) the QR2–KN8 diagonal, (3) the QR1–KR8 diagonal—which Morphy proceeds to seize with his next four moves!

16 P–B4	N–B3
17 B–B4ch	K–R1
18 B–N2	Q–K2
19 QR–K1	R–B3

There is no defense against 20 PxP. If instead 19 . . . PxP; 20 RxP, Q–B3; 21 R–K8!, RxR; 22 QxQ, PxQ; 23 BxP mate.

20 PxP	Q–B1
21 R–K8!	QxR
22 QxR!	Q–K2

Or 22 . . . PxQ; 23 BxP mate.

23 QxPch!	QxQ
24 P–B6	*Black Resigns*

There is no satisfactory defense to P–B7 dis. mate!

The twentieth-century neo-romantics, notably Tchigorin, Marshall and Spielmann, carried Morphy's lessons of the open game to the point of absurdity when they attempted to render Force completely subservient to aesthetics. Marshall, in particular, lacked the ability to discriminate between the beautiful and the possible, often over-reaching himself. The Romantics, in general, suffered from an inability to discipline their imaginations.

The Romantic style was characteristic of the man loving action and quick success. The classical reaction was due principally to the character of one who was disinterested in the glory of ready success, who strove instead for lasting values—Wilhelm Steinitz.

Wilhelm Steinitz and the Classicists: Closed Game

Wilhelm Steinitz (1836–1900) was a chess philosopher who hungered for *essences*. He sought all his life for general laws and loathed exceptions. When he finally revolted against Romantic doctrines, the break was sharp and irrevocable.

Steinitz's doctrinaire spirit sought to rule out all human weakness. If he lost with a particular line, he would continue to try it again and again. This peculiar tropism was due to the belief that his failure to succeed with the line lay in his own human failure. Yet his very success was due to his passionate love of chess, his faith, his tenacity, not to his "system"! It was typical of him to undertake the ungrateful task of a protracted defense for the sake of the most trifling, but permanent, positional advantage. He was the personification of the short term evil versus the long term good. Steinitz strove with might and main to impose order on the Irrational to which the Romantics wholeheartedly surrendered. He made the closed game his special domain because, unlike the open game, which is in constant flux, the closed position is characterized by barricaded Pawn structures and is thus more amenable to systematic approach.

9

Steinitz was the first to realize the necessity of evaluating a position—then *acting* on that evaluation. This objectivity forbade him from entering a speculative combination, and then trusting to luck. It occurred to him that the master should not seek winning combinations unless he can first prove to himself that he holds an advantage. Thus, when his opponent went contrary to the objective demands of the position, Steinitz felt morally impelled to punish the crime. Steinitz himself made no attempt to win in the early stages of the game, as Morphy had done, because he was convinced that this was possible only after his opponent had made an error and not before. So he sought out of the openings minute advantages which gradually added up to one big winning combination. In an age where playing to win from the very start was considered the only honorable course, such a doctrine was assured of a scornful reception. Not surprisingly, all his victories were in fact begrudged.

In 1866 Steinitz wrested the world title from Anderssen, who promptly conceded that Steinitz was even better than Morphy. Yet so bitter was the enmity against Steinitz's style of play that even after he had held the world championship for twenty years, a self-appointed committee of three amateurs claimed that "Morphy could have given Steinitz Pawn and move." And a noted critic once wrote that Steinitz's two match victories over Zukertort were attributable to the fact that "Zukertort was not yet Zukertort in 1872" (the date of their first championship match), "and was no longer Zukertort in 1886" (the date of their second match).

Steinitz held the world title from 1866 until 1894. During this period he was so anxious to vanquish those who scorned his "system" that his style became provocative. Steinitz often invited premature attacks. He made the most unusual moves in order to provoke his adversaries into playing for a win and thus overreaching themselves when the position did not really justify such an attempt. Quite characteristically, Steinitz once wrote, "*A win by an unsound combination, however showy, fills me with artistic horror.*" A winning combination, he was the first to perceive, is possible only after one side has erred. Make no errors, therefore, and one should never lose!

Diagram 6

White moves. *White is a Pawn ahead, but not many players today would care to defend his position. White's King is exposed in the center and has forfeited the right to castle. (Steinitz was so famous for moving his King in the opening that the maneuver came to be known as the "Steinitzian King.") In fact, if it were Black's move, 1 . . . KR–K1 would regain the Pawn with a winning attack. Moreover, White is far behind in development.*

1 N–K1! . . .

This curious move, which seems to take a vital piece out of play, is in reality the only defense. It prepares 2 P–Q3, bolstering the KP and releasing the Q-Bishop. Also, the Knight can later return into play with N–B3, gaining a tempo by the attack on the Queen.

1 . . . **N–QN5**

The idea is to prevent 2 P–Q3 because of NxBP! 3 NxN, QxPch, etc. However, this is no more than a trap, and Black would have been better advised to reconcile himself to the loss of the Pawn by continuing with the positional 1 . . . KR–K1.

2 P–QR3 **KR–K1**

The point of Black's little combination. The retreat of the Knight to B3 would be pointless.

3 PxN **NxP**
4 Q–B5ch! . . .

This is the refutation. Of course not 4 NxN?, RxNch winning the Queen.

4 . . . **K–N1**
5 NxN **RxNch**
6 K–Q1

White was able to withstand the ensuing attack, and eventually he reached the endgame where his material advantage proved decisive.

11

The real question is, why should a position which looks so hopeless at first glance contain so many hidden resources? The main reason is that White's Pawn Structure has no organic weaknesses. Black has a transitory advantage in Time (superior development), but this requires the utmost ingenuity to sustain. Meanwhile, White could not be prevented from consolidating in one move with 1 N–K1! Thus Steinitz's theories approached Philidor's in that he recognized in the elements of Pawn Structure and Force those advantages which *endure* to the end. Steinitz's principal contribution to technique lay in his ability to convert Time and Space into these more durable elements.

Steinitz's theories bore upon something much bigger than chess— namely, life itself, struggle, reason—mirrored in sixty-four squares. His theories could be further elaborated in two directions: philosophically or practically. Emanuel Lasker followed the first lead ("I who vanquished Steinitz must see to it that his great achievement, his theories, should find justice, and I must avenge the wrongs he suffered"). Siegbert Tarrasch took the second lead.

The mantle of classicism thus fell upon Dr. Siegbert Tarrasch, who both enriched and impoverished Steinitz's teachings by selecting only the portion which appealed to his own temperament. (For example, Tarrasch preferred mobility plus a weakness to constricted positions without weaknesses.) Today these teachings are the stock in trade of every player from Grandmaster to Grandpatzer: occupy the center, fortify it, seek mobility and minute advantages, play with a plan. Tarrasch elaborated all this with a clarity and simplicity that remain masterly to this day. Even today, in the pictures which have been passed down to us, one can sense the arrogance of this stiffly posed German doctor. That his dogmatism should irk the younger generation is not surprising.

And that there should be a reaction against this starchy pedanticism was inevitable. It remained only for the younger masters to express it openly after World War I.

Réti and the Hypermoderns: Flank Game

The hypermoderns were thoroughgoing iconoclasts, and today it seems no accident that they rose to prominence after a World War which ravaged all established values and conventions. They attacked their classical heritage on the grounds that no two chess positions are ever quite identical, that the so-called "rules" and "general principles" result in "automatic chess" when applied indiscriminately.

The two schools immediately came into conflict on a crucial matter: the center. *Occupation*, argued the classicists, was imperative.

Control, countered the hypermoderns, was the real necessity. Accordingly, they sought openings which allowed their opponents a free hand in the center, only to cripple it later with deft blows from the flanks. Their insouciance was remarkable. Breyer once began annotating a game by giving 1 P–K4 a question mark, accompanied by the comment that "White's game is in its last throes!" Why? Well, he argued, 1 P–K4 does not actually develop a piece (it merely prepares development by opening lines); furthermore, White has committed himself irretrievably in the center by creating a target. There must be a way to attack this target, even to *provoke* White into advancing and providing more targets. Alekhine's Defense fitted this prescription: **1 P–K4, N–KB3; 2 P–K5, N–Q4; 3 P–QB4, N–N3; 4 P–Q4.** Black's Knight has been driven from pillar to post, but White has made no developing moves in the meantime—on the contrary, he has occupied the center to his own detriment. White has been transformed into a flat-footed opponent squaring away with his feet planted firmly in the center of the ring, while Black bobs and weaves and jabs from all directions to his heart's content. At present, White is thought to maintain a slight advantage in Space and Time which offsets his weakness in Pawn Structure. The Black Knight on QN3 is misplaced, and serves no function other than provoking White's central flurry.

Diagram 7

Is White's center strong or weak? This "chase variation" puts the soundness of the defense to its most severe test: **4 . . . P–Q3; 5 P–B4** (the "Four Pawns Attack"), **PxP; 6 BPxP, N–B3; 7 B–K3** (timing is important. Not 7 N–B3, B–N5 with severe pressure on the center), **B–B4; 8 N–QB3, P–K3; 9 N–B3, Q–Q2; 10 B–K2, O–O–O; 11 O–O** and White's center is still intact, serving its original function by cramping Black's game. Still, many masters distrust this advanced center, and the modern tendency is to omit P–QB4 and develop a piece instead: viz., **1 P–K4, N–KB3; 2 P–K5, N–Q4; 3 P–Q4, P–Q3; 4 N–KB3, B–N5; 5 B–K2.**

13

Since the opening is a struggle for domination of the center, the hypermoderns sought a system which put direct pressure on it from the flank without fixing the central Pawns too soon. The natural opening move in such a system is **1 N–KB3** which, moreover, does not commit the first player.

The moves of the hypermoderns were not always new, though the principles behind them were. "The Opening of the future," as Tartakower dubbed the Réti-Zukertort opening in 1924, had been played as far back as 1804 by Napoleon Bonaparte!

The principles of the "chess cubists" were put to their most grueling test at the N.Y. International Tournament in 1924. The following, from the game Réti-Yates, is a quite typical hypermodern position.

Diagram 8

Black moves. *Black's Pawns occupy the center. Meanwhile, White exerts pressure on them by having placed his Queen on a most bizarre square. The game continued:*

| **1 . . .** | N(1)–Q2 |

To protect the threatened KP.

| **2 KR–B1** | P–KR3 |

It soon becomes obvious that White has to regroup his pieces because, having reached his maximum, he has nowhere else to go. Black already has too much momentum in the center; White must constantly guard against P–K5.

Eventually it became obvious that the hypermoderns allowed their opponents too much leeway in the center. The great contribution of the hypermodern school is in pointing out that on many occasions an advantage in Space is incompatible with an advantage in Pawn Structure. The school fell into disrepute because it failed to discriminate as it destroyed. It negated the best along with the worst of the classical heritage. There was, of course, an historical reason for their sweeping exaggeration. Classical theory was so entrenched by the time they appeared on the scene that the hypermoderns were forced to overstate their case in order to be heard. By bending the stick to one side, they helped to place it in the middle. Their imperishable message is to keep our eyes open, to avoid routine, and to approach each position with an open mind.

The Technicians: Neo-Classical School

The technicians are what the word implies: they "play like a book in the opening, like a magician in the mid-game, and like a machine in the ending." Like Steinitz, they rarely try to force the game or go contrary to the objective demands of the position. As a general rule, in closed games, Space is more important than Time. This lends itself to positions where patience and endless maneuvering are the order of the day. It is really remarkable what the good technician can do once he is given the most minute advantage. Exploiting weak squares and accumulating invisible advantages are matters of second nature. They have absorbed all the knowledge of the past, and apply to it unparalleled technique. Their emphasis is on how to win a won game rather than on how to get one.

Because of the slow jockeying for position so characteristic of their games, the technicians are continually reproached with being dull and colorless. The average player is not equipped with the patience or the ability to appreciate this subtle brand of chess in which all the action seems to take place beneath the surface. Nothing "happens," no slam-bang attacks, no flim-flam—yet somehow the technicians emerge triumphant. At Carlsbad, 1929, Rubinstein extracted a win from such a "hopelessly drawn" Rook and Pawn ending that the editors of the tournament book united in the assertion that had this happened three hundred years ago Rubinstein would have been burned at the stake for being in league with evil spirits!

The great technicians—past and present—include such illustrious names as Rubinstein, Capablanca, Reshevsky, Smyslov, and Flohr. They make few errors and lose few games. When they are beaten, it is usually in a manner which reflects credit on their opponents. It goes without saying that they are hard to beat. The way to pick out the technicians in scanning the cross-table of a tournament is to look for those players with the greatest number of draws. The technician is generally content to draw with players of his own class, while beating the weaker players with monotonous regularity. One seldom hears of an "upset." At the Kemeri Tournament in 1937 Flohr tied for first place with a score of 12–5 which comprised 7 wins and 10 draws—all the more remarkable because these draws were against the very next ten players in the standing!

Asked whether he expected to win the U.S. Western Tournament in 1933, Reshevsky replied, "Who is there to beat me?" Nobody did beat him—but he didn't win the tournament. Too many draws. In *Meet the Masters*, Euwe writes: "Reshevsky often wins with Black; there arise lively positions in which his tactical preparedness counts for a lot." This is an apt observation. Technicians prefer counter-attack to attack, baring their claws only when provoked. They prefer their opponents to take the initiative. The reason they draw with each other so frequently is that neither side is willing to take risks. Perhaps this style is not held in high esteem because the general public senses a basic lack of courage.

Economy

"No second chance!" is the battle-cry of the technicians. Economy —the execution of a given end in a minimum number of moves— is their trade mark. They are masters of the finesse, the interpolation. Nothing escapes them—not the slightest transposition.

KRAMER—BISGUIER, ROSENWALD TOURNEY, NEW YORK, 1955–56

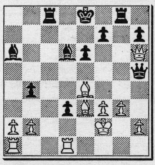

Diagram 9

Black moves. *Black must force White to relinquish the blockade on K3, and the slightest transposition of moves can lose him the precious initiative. The transition from this to the next diagram is accomplished by Bisguier without the batting of an eyelash!*

1 . . .	R–B7ch!

Accurate! Not 1 . . . QxQ; 2 BxQ, R–B7ch; 3 R–Q2, RxRch (or . . . B–B4ch; 4 K–K1!); 4 BxR, B–B4ch; 5 K–B3—and White maintains the blockade.

2 R–Q2	RxRch
3 BxR	B–B4ch

Again more accurate than 3 . . . QxQ; 4 BxQ, B–B4ch; 5 B–K3.
The point is 4 B–K3 now loses to QxQ.

4	K–N2	QxQ
5	BxQ	P–B4
6	B–B6ch	K–K2
7	R–Q1	P–K4
8	B–Q2	K–Q3
9	B–R4	B–B5
10	B–N3	. . .

Or if 10 P–N3, B–R3 and White's K–Bishop is locked out of play.

10	. . .	BxB
11	PxB	K–Q4
12	B–K1	P–K5
13	B–B2	BxB
14	KxB	K–Q5

Diagram 10

Position after 14 . . . K–Q5

White resigns. *He is defenseless against . . . P–K6ch. (Finally
Black has won the vital K6 square.) The two passed Pawns are
enough to make Columbus sorry he discovered America.*

The Eclectics

The eclectics have inherited the Romantic tradition, derived from
Morphy, and they have fortified it with a century of chess technique.
They are primarily tacticians—alert to every possibility, courageous,
original, sharp. While the technician steers for positions which are
nearly always under his control (preferably where he can keep the
draw in hand), the tactician surrenders himself to complications.

While the technician strives for closed positions, the tactician strives for open games where everything hangs by a hair. The technician aims for the endgame (because he prefers positions which respond to technique rather than to imagination). The tactician concentrates on opening theory, always seeking new ways to introduce a sharp and early battle. The difference is primarily one of temperament.

In 1951, after drawing a world title match with Botvinnik, Bronstein admitted that he threw away several very critical endgames. It seems he lost patience with these relatively "dull" positions!

If one word could summarize the present renaissance of Soviet chess, it would be "dynamism." (One wonders to what extent the values of a culture are reflected in its chess.) The leading exponents of the eclectic school have derived mainly from that geographical region: Alekhine, Bronstein, Keres, Geller, and to some extent, Botvinnik, whose style resembles Emanuel Lasker's. It goes without saying that the distinction between the classical and eclectic schools is not always self-evident, inasmuch as a tactician may often find himself playing positional chess, and vice versa. Keres' style, for instance, has undergone a marked drift toward neo-classicism.

The eclectics dislike symmetrical positions because of their drawing tendencies. They seek at all times double-edged moves which introduce imbalance, thereby stamping a definite character on the game. The following illustration is quite typical.

BISGUIER—EVANS, ROSENWALD TOURNAMENT, NEW YORK, 1955–56

Diagram 11

Black moves. *Black's QBP is attacked. The insipid 1 . . . PxP meets this threat, but after 2 PxP White will have freed his Q-Bishop and the game will assume a drawish character because of the balanced Pawn Structure. Black must seek a way to maintain the tension if he wants to produce winning chances. This he can do with* **1 . . . P–B5; 2 B–B2, R–K1.** *Now Black has created a Q-side majority; the Pawn Structure is imbalanced. (Black has 3 Pawns to*

2 *on the Q-side, and it is always easier to force a passed Pawn in
the endgame with 3 against 2 than with 5 against 4.)* The consequent
struggle will be over White's attempt to force P–K4 while Black tries
to restrain this (*the reason for* 2 . . . *R–K1*) *and mobilize his own
Q-side majority in the meantime. Black's chances are better because
White's pieces are momentarily entangled. The game, however, was
eventually drawn.*

Sharpness

"Sharpness" is a combination of alertness and precision. It is
characterized by the relentless search for hidden resources and a
disdain for the "obvious" move. Even if there are a thousand good
reasons for rejecting a given move, the tactician is always ready to
consider it, and he often gains an advantage in this totally unexpected
way. The position that follows is incredibly complicated, everything
is suspended in mid-air, Black's Rook is *en prise*, yet the master-
magician, Alekhine, pulls all the strings. One slip by Black and
White will have time to consolidate. Alekhine finds one stroke after
another, each more powerful than the last, so that his harassed
opponent is given no breathing space.

RÉTI—ALEKHINE, BADEN-BADEN, 1925

Diagram 12

Black moves.

	1 . . .	N–B6!

Black counterattacks—ignoring his attacked Rook.

	2 QxP	. . .

Forced. 2 Q–B4 is met by P–QN4 and the Queen must relinquish
its guard of the KP.

	2 . . .	QxQ
	3 NxQ	NxPch
	4 K–R2	. . .

19

4 K–B1, NxPch; 5 PxN, BxN leaves Black a Pawn ahead with a winning position. Now White seems safe, for if 4 . . . NxR; 5 PxR holds everything. How can Black sustain his initiative?

Diagram 13

Position after 4 K–R2

4 . . .	N–K5!!

A marvellous stroke—and the only move to maintain the initiative. Even without Queens on the board the battle rages fiercely.

5 R–B4	. . .

Réti finds the very best defense. Not 5 PxR, NxR (7) and if 6 NxN, NxR winning the exchange.

5 . . .	NxBP!

And not 5 . . . NxR; 6 NxN; R–QB6; 7RxB. Or 5 . . . BxN; 6 RxN (4)! The prosaic text seems to end all the fireworks. The win of a Pawn is not in itself sufficient to win, but Black still has a winning mid-game attack.

The remaining moves were: **6 B–N2, B–K3; 7 R(B4)–B2, N–N5ch; 8 K–R3 (not 8 K–R1, R–R8ch), N–K4 dis. ch; 9 K–R2, RxN; 10 RxN, N–N5ch; 11 K–R3, N–K6 dis. ch; 12 K–R2, NxR; 13 BxR, N–Q5!** *White Resigns.* For if now 14 R–K3, NxBch; 15 RxN, B–Q4 wins a piece.

Diagram 14

__White moves.__ __He has a sharp interpolation.__ An unimaginative player, intent on repairing Force, might play 1 QxP, which gives Black time for P–Q3, assuring him of free and easy development. If White is to sustain his initiative, he must first see to it that Black does not get his pieces out. Hence the interpolation—

1 P–K5!! · · ·

A sharp move which virtually wins by force. Black's game is now extremely difficult. If 1 . . . P–Q3; 2 P–QN4 (to divert the Bishop from a defensive diagonal: QR6–KB1), B–N3; 3 B–KN5 leads to a strong attack. Still, this is Black's best practical chance. The defense chosen in the game leads to a massacre.

1 . . . **P–KR3**

Black loses more Time, in order to prevent B–KN5. Now White's Q-Bishop heads for an even more devastating diagonal. Of course not 1 . . . NxP; 2 NxN, QxN; 3 R–K1.

2 P–QN4	**B–N3**
3 P–QR4	**P–QR4**
4 B–R3	· · ·

Already Black is without an adequate defense. If 4 . . . PxP; 5 PxP, NxNP; 6 Q–N3, B–B4; 7 N–B3 and it is impossible for Black to get his pieces out. The threat is BxN followed by N–Q5. If 7 . . . P–QB3; 8 N–K4 wins material.

21

CHAPTER TWO: Pawn Structure

In some primers, with good reason, endgames are taught first—
though the novice rarely is made to comprehend why. "Pawn
endings are to chess what putting is to golf," observed Purdy.
More than this—Pawn Structure is to chess what cell structure is to
life. After a handful of moves the chessmaster already is evaluating
his position in terms of his endgame prospects. Should he play to
simplify and exchange pieces? Should he play for an attack instead?
Let's digress a bit—it's really germane—to see how this works.

The Outside Passed Pawn

Consider the basic principle of many King and Pawn endgames—
"when there are no outside passed Pawns, every effort must be made
to create one." If the Pawn Structure is balanced, of course, this is
quite impossible. That is why, for example, if each side has six
Pawns, masters generally will make some attempt in the very opening
to force 3 against 2 on the Q's side (see "Q's Side Majority"), and
3 against 4 on the K-side—rather than a straight 3 against 3 on each
wing. The reason is that it is technically easier to create an outside
passed Pawn with 3 against 2 than with 4 against 3.

Diagram 15

White wins. He has an outside passed Pawn.

Here the forces are so reduced and the material so even that one is tempted perfunctorily to dismiss the position as a draw. If anything, Black seems to have the more active King. However, the presence of White's tiny QBP—the outside passed Pawn—is the decisive factor. The principle involved is that Black must rush his King headlong in front of White's QBP in order to block its queening path, whereupon, at the proper moment, White will pitch or sacrifice this Pawn and (in the process) march his King to the remaining Black Pawns on the K's wing and remove them all.

Black to move, the game proceeded: **1 . . . P–R4; 2 P–R4, P–K4; 3 P–B3ch, K–K5** (3 . . . K–B5; 4 K–B2, K–Q4; 5 K–Q3 eventually forces Black to give ground); **4 K–K2, P–N3; 5 K–Q2** (note how White marks time while Black exhausts his remaining Pawn moves, whereupon his King will have to give way), **K–B5** (Black is trying desperately to dissolve his K-side Pawns before returning with his King to the Q's wing, so that when White marches his King to the K-side there will be no Pawns for him to gobble. This defense fails due to lack of Time); **6 K–Q3, P–N4; 7 PxP, KxP; 8 K–K4, K–B3; 9 K–Q5!** (not the hasty 9 P–B4?, K–K3; 10 P–B5, P–R5; 11 P–B6, K–Q3; 12 P–B7—the pitch—KxP; 13 KxP, K–Q2; 14 K–B5, P–R6!; 15 PxP, K–K2—*draw*—the RP cannot win when the opposing King gets in front of it), **K–B4; 10 P–B4,** and now if **P–K5; 11 K–Q4!, K–B5; 12 P–B5, P–K6; 13 K–Q3, K–K4; 14 KxP, K–Q4; 15 K–B4, KxP; 16 K–N5, K–Q4; 17 KxP—*White wins.***

Pawn Structure Determines Strategy

Armed with this previous example, we are now in a position to consider the exchange variation of the Ruy Lopez after seven standard moves: **1 P–K4, P–K4; 2 N–KB3, N–QB3; 3 B–N5, P–QR3; 4 BxN, QPxB; 5 P–Q4, PxP; 6 QxP, QxQ; 7 NxQ.**

Diagram 16

White has a winning Pawn structure but—. This position contains many basic principles and many exceptions. For the nonce let us content ourselves with the following observations: (a) in effect White is a Pawn ahead on the K-side (Black's doubled QBP's are worthless; his 4 Q-side Pawns are held in check by White's 3. To satisfy yourself remove all the pieces from the board and try to create a Queen with one of the Black Pawns); (b) as a result of his superior Pawn Structure White has a forced win in the endgame; therefore, (c) each exchange brings him closer to victory.

This, then, is White's strategy—to swap pieces at each and every opportunity. The fly in the ointment is that chess is a game of conflict—dynamic, not static. Black has compensation in other elements (the 2 Bishops). "Before the ending the gods have placed the middle game," said Tarrasch, to explain just such positions as these, where one side has a winning advantage in the ending *if he can ever get to it*. Right now the important thing to note is the similarity, *in principle*, of this diagram to the previous one. To do this, mentally sweep all the pieces off the board except the Kings. It will look like this—

White wins by creating a passed Pawn on the K-Side. There is no point in outlining the solution here. It may require 20—perhaps 30 moves—but that is a problem of endgame technique. The winning process consists of creating a passed Pawn on the K-side. Note only that if the Black Pawn were on Q3, instead of QB3, the game would be a theoretical draw.

Diagram 17

Diagram 18

The ideal Pawn structure

Pawn Mobility

"Pawn mobility" refers to the Pawn's relative power to advance. In our discussion of the outside passed Pawn we saw that its great power lay in its ability to advance, unimpeded by enemy Pawns. We are thus in a position to draw our first tentative conclusion: *Pawns that are free to advance are healthier than Pawns that are unable to do so.* The point where every Pawn has equal mobility exists in the original structure.

This is ideal because neither side has any weakness, and all the Pawns are ready to offer fraternal support to each other. The Hypermoderns were the first to understand the real value of this original Pawn Structure, but they went to extremes in trying to keep it intact. Certain Pawns—the central ones preferably—must be advanced, courageously, in order to get the pieces out and establish beachheads. The remaining Pawns should stand duty as reserves. But remember—reserves can be called upon only once in every game. So use them sparingly, and not at all if possible.

Every time a Pawn is advanced it loses some of its mobility. It crosses that metaphysical boundary which divides *essence* from *being.* The original Pawn Structure is healthy because it possesses absolute mobility, absolute flexibility, absolute potential.

25

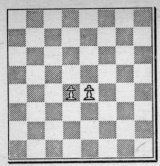

Diagram 19

Mobile Pawns

Diagram 20

Semi-mobile Pawns

Mobile Pawns are the most desirable formation. White's center Pawns are free to advance without being hindered by enemy Pawns on the same file. They can be stopped only by a blockade with enemy pieces.

Semi-mobile Pawns are free to advance, but only relatively: as soon as they advance, they lose their mobility. Thus if P–K5, P–Q4 locks the formation. And if 1 P–Q5, P–K4. While after 1 P–Q5, PxP; 2 PxP, neither Pawn is free to advance any further.

Diagram 21

Immobile Pawns

A Pawn is *immobile* when it is physically unable to advance. For practical purposes Pawns may also be considered immobile where they are free to advance, but where to do so would cause their loss without any corresponding compensation. A backward Pawn on an open file is a good example.

Try to mobilize center Pawns

Diagram 22

White moves. Despite hypermodern dogma, occupation of the center more often than not also means control—especially when the center Pawns are mobile.

White must play to force P–K4 even though this would weaken his QP. It is the only way to open lines for his Q-Bishop and to free his game. Note the elaborate measure each side has taken for and against P–K4. Can White play it yet?

WHITE	BLACK	WHITE	BLACK
1 P–K4	PxP	8 K–B1	N–KN5
2 PxP	B–KN5	9 N–Q3	B–N3
3 Q–Q3	N–K3	10 B–B4	QR–Q1
4 P–R3[1]	QxPch!	11 K–K2	N–Q5ch[2]
5 QxQ	NxQ	12 K–Q2	N–N6ch
6 PxB	N–B7	13 K–K2	N–Q5ch
7 P–N5	B–B4ch		*Draw*

[1] Safer is 4 B–K3, reinforcing the center and threatening P–R3.

[2] 11 . . . NxQR; 12 RxN favors White—two pieces are nearly always better than a Rook (see "Force"). There is no way for White to avert the perpetual check without material loss. If, for instance, 14 K–B1, N–B7; 15 QR–Q1, N(5)–K6ch; 16 K–K2, NxB wins for Black. On 14 K–Q1, N–N6 White will be in trouble if he plays anything but K–B2; therefore, he accepts the draw after N–Q5ch.

Play for the "steamroller"

EVANS—LARSEN, U.S. OPEN CHAMPIONSHIP, 1949

Diagram 23

Black moves. The "steamroller" consists of two or more connected Pawns in the center which are so highly mobile that one or the other is constantly threatening to advance, like molten lava.

The best defense is to try and provoke one or the other Pawn to advance, so that a line of defense (or a blockade) can be established.

WHITE	BLACK	WHITE	BLACK
1 . . .	N–K4[1]	7 Q–B3	P–B4
2 B–N5	N–B3	8 Q–R5!	R–KN1
3 P–Q5	Q–K4	9 R–R3	Q–N2
4 BxN	PxB	10 R–B2	P–B5?
5 R–K3	N–K2	11 Q–R6![2]	
6 R–N3ch	K–R1		

[1] In order to reach B3 and thus force the Pawn to advance to Q5. The alternative, P–KR3, would prevent White's next move, but create a weakness. Black tries to force White to play P–Q5 so that he can set up a blockade on the dark squares (K4 and Q3). White's steamroller, reinforced by the two Bishops, is already too formidable, however.

[2] Leading to a won endgame because of Black's indefensible KBP. This is a very instructive example of Pawn Structure converted into attack, then re-converted at the proper moment back into Pawn Structure. Black loses this endgame due to his hopeless Pawn Structure.

The remaining moves were: 11 . . . B–B1; 12 QxQch, RxQ; 13 QR–B3, N–N3; 14 R–Q2, P–B3; 15 R(3)–B2, B–Q2; 16 N–K2, P–B6; 17 RxP, N–R5; 18 R–KB2, QR–KN1; 19 N–N3, P–KR4; 20 RxP, R–N4; 21 P–K5, RxP; 22 R–R6ch, K–N2; 23 R–R7ch, K–B1; 24 RxB, R–K8ch; 25 K–B2, RxB; 26 R–QB7, R–N5; 27 P–Q6, R–B5ch; 28 K–K3, N–N3; 29 P–Q7, R–N6ch; 30 K–K2, Black Resigns.

Majorities must be mobilized

Black moves. White threatens P–QN3, setting up a blockade on QB4. If Black permits this, his Q-side majority will be stopped cold. Somehow, Black must activate his seemingly immobile QBP.

Note Black's Q-side majority (3 to 2), whereas White is virtually a Pawn down because of his doubled King Pawns.

Diagram 24

WHITE	BLACK	WHITE	BLACK
1 ...	P–B5!	2 QxQ[1]	NxQ[2]

[1] No better is 2 RxP?, QxQ; 3 PxQ, RxR. Black's timing is important. He could not first play 1 . . . QxQ; 2 PxQ, P–B5 because of 3 RxRP.

[2] White is lost. His doubled K-Pawns are worthless, and Black has a bind. It is only a question of time before he invades on the Q-file. White's QR is tied to the defense of the QRP; his other pieces are fatally ensnared.

Perhaps White's hopelessness can be more fully appreciated if we follow the game for awhile: 3 K–B1, P–R4; 4 P–K4, R–Q5; 5 K–K2, P–N3; 6 B–Q2, B–B4; 7 B–K3, R–Q2; 8 BxB, RxB; 9 P–KN3, R–B1; 10 R–Q1, QR–Q1; 11 P–R3, RxR; 12 NxR, R–Q6; 13 N–K3, R–Q5; 14 N–B2, R–Q6; 15 N–K3, R–N6; 16 R–R2, K–B1; 17 P–N4, P–R5; 18 P–B5, P–N4; 19 K–Q2, K–K1; 20 K–K2, K–Q2; 21 R–R1 (or White can wait for strangulation), RxPch, with an easy win for Black.

Semi-mobile center Pawns

EVANS—SANDRIN, U.S. CHAMPIONSHIP, 1948

White moves. White's KP seems to be immobile because its advance apparently loses a Pawn without any compensation.

The real blockader is Black's Pawn on Q3. In order to mobilize, White must demolish this blockade. This he can do owing to a tactical possibility. How?

Diagram 25

WHITE	BLACK	WHITE	BLACK
1 P–K5!!	PxP[1]	2 B–R7![2]	

[1] There is nothing better. If instead 1 . . . NxKP; 2 B–N6 wins the Queen! Or if 1 . . . NxQP White has several good moves, of which probably 2 P–K6 is the best. Finally, if 1 . . . N–K1; 2 P–K6 wins material. When Pawns are semi-mobile, as in this case, one must be alert to the tactical implications.

[2] White wins the exchange, owing to the double threat of P–Q6 and BxR. An alternative to the text is 2 P–Q6, QxP; 3 BxP.

It is extraordinary how quickly Black falls apart once it is possible for White to mobilize his KP. This often happens to cramped positions as soon as the lines are opened.

Passed Pawns

Diagram 26

White has a passed QP. A passed Pawn *has no enemy Pawns either directly in front, or adjacent to it. It may be either a source of strength or a source of weakness, depending upon its mobility. In the endgame it acquires power because its queening path must be blocked by the opposing King, leaving its own King free for other dirty work (as in diagram* 15).

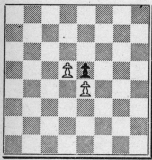

Diagram 27

White has a protected passed QP. The protected passed Pawn *is always a strong formation. It has all the desirable attributes of the passed Pawn, and is, in addition, self-sufficient. The only way to attack it is to undermine its base (in this case, the Pawn on K*4).

Diagram 28

White has a potential passed QP. A Pawn is potentially passed *when the enemy Pawn on an adjacent file can be cleared away by a simple exchange. In this case White could have an actual passed QP by the simple process of playing* 1 P–Q5, PxP; 2 PxP.

Passed Pawns must be pushed!

EVANS—R. BYRNE, WERTHEIM MEMORIAL, NEW YORK, 1951

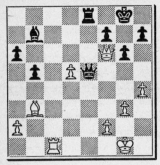

White moves. The passed Pawn can be a mighty weapon even in the middle game if it is not blockaded and if it is backed up by major pieces. In short, a passed Pawn which is also mobile constitutes a tangible advantage because when it is pushed far enough, the enemy will have to sacrifice a piece in order to prevent it from queening. (*See also diagram 32.*)

Diagram 29

WHITE	BLACK	WHITE	BLACK
1 QxQ	**RxQ**	**3 P–Q7**	**R–Q1**
2 P–Q6![1]	**R–K1**	**4 R–B7**	***Black Resigns[2]***

[1] With the powerful threat of P–Q7. Nimzovitch indulged in a quaint "pathetic fallacy" when he attributed the onward movement of a passed Pawn to its "lust to expand."
[2] Black must lose at least a Bishop, with more to follow. If 4 . . . B–K5; 5 R–B8 forces a new Queen. And, of course, 4 . . . R–N1 is met by 5 RxB, RxR; 6 P–Q8=Qch.

Clear the path for passed Pawns. Demolish blockades.

EVANS—BISGUIER, U.S. OPEN CHAMPIONSHIP, 1950

Diagram 30

Black moves. We have already determined that the strength of a passed Pawn depends upon its mobility. Here Black's QBP apparently is immobile because of White's staunch blockade on QB1. Exchanging Knights will do no good because Black has no other piece which can exert pressure on that square. White threatens 1 NxN, BxNch; 2 K–Q2! So it is obvious that Black must use his precious move to solve the problem by combinative means.

WHITE	BLACK	WHITE	BLACK
1 ...	R–QR1!	5 B–N2[4]	NxB
2 RxR[1]	NxNch	6 K–Q2	N–Q8
3 K–K3[2]	N–Q6![3]	7 R–R4	N–B6
4 B–R3	P–N5	8 R–R1[5]	K–R3

White resigns. He is in "Zugzwang."*

[1] What else? The Rook cannot remain on the rank.
[2] Forced. Not 2 K–Q2?, NxPch and the Pawn queens next.
[3] 3 . . . NxP; 4 B–R3, P–N5; 5 B–N2, P–B8(Q)ch; 6 BxQ, NxB; 7 R–QN8, N–Q6; 8 P–B4 gives White drawing chances.
[4] K–Q2 is refuted by N–B4!!—a beautiful final point.
[5] Or if 8 RxP, P–B8(Q)ch; 9 KxQ, N–R7ch winning the Rook.

---

* "*Zugzwang*" means the unpleasant obligation to move.

Create protected passed Pawns

Black moves. This position represents a theoretical balance: White's Bishop and Knight tally 70 units against Rook and two Pawns—also 70. (See "Table of Relative Values".) Black's Pawn Structure is bad. His QP's are doubled and his RP is attacked. He must find some way to unparalyze his Pawns.

Diagram 31

WHITE	BLACK	WHITE	BLACK
1 . . .	P–Q6ch![1]	5 K–B2	K–R6
2 PxP[2]	P–N6	6 N–K2	P–N8(Q)ch!
3 K–Q2	K–N5	7 KxQ	R–QN2
4 B–N6	P–N7	8 N–B3	RxBch[3]

[1] Black cannot stop to defend. This is the only way to sustain the initiative. If instead 1 . . . K–B5; 2 BxP, K–B6; 3 K–Q1, followed by N–K2ch.

[2] Disagreeably forced. Now 2 KxP is met by R–B6ch, winning the Knight. Black now has a protected passed QNP.

[3] Having won material, the rest is easy for Black.

Mobilize potential passed Pawns

EUWE—EVANS, WERTHEIM MEMORIAL, NEW YORK, 1951

Diagram 32

Black moves. Black has a semi-mobile Q-side Pawn mass coupled with control of the open QR file. His QBP is potentially passed. The problem is to force a passed Pawn in such a manner that it will be decisive. There are several ways to accomplish this. Note that Black's extraordinary Pawn mobility more than compensates for the Pawn which he is behind. Here is a case where Pawn Structure outweighs a disadvantage in Force.

WHITE	BLACK	WHITE	BLACK
1 . . .	P–N6[1]	5 PxB	N–N5
2 P–Q5[2]	NxP	6 K–B4	K–B2[3]
3 B–Q4	PxP	7 B–K5	N–B7[4]
4 N–B6ch	BxN		

[1] The immediate 1 . . . P–B6 is also good, but the text is a trifle sharper. This order of moves gains Time because White must stop to defend his QRP.

[2] A desperate bid to free his pieces. If instead 2 P–QR3, P–B6!; 3 PxP, N–B5; 4 B–B4, RxP followed by P–N7.

[3] Safer than 6 . . . N–B7; 7 R–N1ch. Now White has no good defense against N–B7. 7 R–KN1 is met by P–R8(Q).

[4] Black wins. This is a good example of converting Pawn Structure into Force.

Connected, isolated and backward Pawns

Diagram 33

Connected Pawns

Connected Pawns are a strong formation because they are in a position to provide mutual defense. Connected Pawns may be either mobile or immobile, depending upon the array of the enemy units opposing them. Pawns on adjacent files which are in a position to defend each other, when advanced, are connected.

Diagram 34

Disconnected or isolated Pawns

Isolated Pawns ("isolanis") are generally weak because they provide an immobile target and are susceptible to blockade. They must be defended with pieces, which is highly uneconomical. Isolated Pawns may be passed or not, again depending upon the placement of the opposing units. The distinguishing characteristic of an isolated Pawn is that there is *no Pawn of the same color on either adjacent file behind it.*

Diagram 35

White's QP is artificially iso-lated. *A Pawn is* artificially isolated *when the Pawn (or Pawns) next to it cannot immediately spring to its defense. It differs from an isolated Pawn in that it* does *have Pawns on either, or both, adjacent files.*

Diagram 36

Black's QP is backward. *We generally think of a Pawn as having become isolated when it has advanced too far beyond the ken of the other Pawns. However, there is also the case of the Pawn which is isolated because it has not advanced far enough. This we term the* backward *Pawn. Note that it meets all the qualifications of an isolated Pawn inasmuch as it has* no *Pawn of the same color on an adjacent file in back of it.*

Diagram 37

Black's QP is backward on an open file. *A* backward Pawn on an open file *is an even more glaring weakness than a simple isolated Pawn because the enemy forces now have access to it via the open file. The main difference is this: while the backward Pawn is physically unable to advance, the backward Pawn on an open file is free to do so, but at the cost of its life.*

Blockade isolated Pawns

BOULACHANIS (GREECE)—EVANS (U.S.A.), OLYMPICS, DUBROVNIK, 1950

White moves. An isolated Pawn is weak for two reasons: (1) it cannot be defended by another Pawn; (2) it cannot control the square directly in front of it—and on this square it can be blockaded. Once an "isolani" has been anaesthetized by means of a blockade, it throws all the other pieces on the defensive.

Diagram 33

WHITE	BLACK	WHITE	BLACK
1 Q–Q3[1]	BxN	6 K–R1	B–B7[3]
2 QxB	RxP	7 KR–K4	R–Q1
3 R–K1	R–Q7[2]	8 R–B1	N–K6
4 P–B3	N–Q4	9 B–Q3	Q–N4
5 R–B4	B–B4ch	10 P–N4	Q–R5

White Resigns

[1] This loses the QP without a fight. Relatively better is 1 B–B4 which momentarily saves the QP and draws some of the poison by forcing Black to part with his beautifully centralized Bishop. After 1 . . . BxB; 2 RxB, R–Q3 followed by QR–Q1 and N–B4 White's isolated QP is still subject to fierce pressure, though it is possible that with perfect defense White can still draw. But that is all he can do—defend. This is the drawback of possessing an immobile isolated Pawn. Incidentally, 1 N–Q7 would not do, owing to the reply, Q–N4, winning a piece.

[2] Black has a powerful initiative in addition to his material advantage. It is amazing how quickly White's game disintegrates.

[3] White is weak on his black squares. Notice how Black invades on this weak square complex.

Try to keep isolated Pawns mobile

EVANS—BISGUIER, TRIANGULAR MATCH, NEW YORK, 1955

Black moves. We have seen the consequences of a blockaded, isolated Pawn in the previous example. An isolani is strong under two conditions: (1) if it exerts a cramping influence on enemy developments; (2) if it can be liquidated at will. Both of these conditions are fulfilled in this position.

Diagram 39

WHITE	BLACK	WHITE	BLACK
1 . . .	P–Q5[1]	4 QxN	BxB
2 PxP	NxP	5 QxB	Q–N3
3 N–N5[2]	NxBch	Drawn[3]	

[1] There is actually no rush to dissolve the isolani so soon. White is in no position to institute a blockade on his Q4 (as, for instance, if his Knight were on Q4 instead of QB3) so Black should take advantage of the lull to develop with 1 . . . R–K1. As long as Black's QP is liquid (can safely advance to Q5) it should be left where it is to cramp White as long as possible.

[2] Active defense is called for. Already Black's pieces are climbing all over the center. If 3 B–Q3, B–N5 is hard to meet.

[3] Black has a slight edge (Bishop and Knight vs. two Knights), but this is very slight indeed. The balanced Pawn Structure assures a draw. Since neither side expects the other to make any mistakes, and since White has lost his theoretical opening advantage of the first move, there is nothing more to play for.

Try to repair isolated Pawns

EVANS—POSCHEL, U.S. CHAMPIONSHIP, 1948

White moves. The principle of repairing weaknesses holds true for Time and Space as well as Pawn Structure. White had been seeking a way throughout this game to eliminate his laggard KP. This gave rise to an alert combination based on the momentary pin of Black's QP. What is it?

Diagram 40

WHITE	BLACK	WHITE	BLACK
1 P-K5!	NxP[1]	4 BxB	P-B4[2]
2 NxN	BxN	5 Q-KB4!	*Black Resigns*[3]
3 RxRch	QxR		

[1] This loses a piece. 1 . . . P-B4 also fails to 2 Q-N6, PxP; 3 RxN!, RxR; 4 N-Q6ch, etc. Relatively best is 1 . . . R-Q1; 2 PxP, NxP, though 3 R-K3 gives White an advantage in Space, and eventually in Pawn Structure, after 3 . . . Q-B3; 4 BxN, PxB; 5 N-N6ch, K-N1; 6 N-Q5.

[2] Black had relied on this move, thinking it would regain the piece.

[3] White now wins a piece. This is a case where, as so very often happens, tactics supplement strategy. White's long-range strategy was to get rid of his isolated KP. Tactics presented him with the proper moment to do so.

Pile up on targets

White moves. Black's isolated QRP is a "target" in the direct firing line of an open QR file. In the endgame this very QRP would be decisive! (Take all the pieces off the board except the King: 1 . . . P–QR4 wins.) Before the ending, however, the gods have placed the middle game. And here White's major pieces are in an ideal position to exploit the target.

Diagram 41

WHITE	BLACK	WHITE	BLACK
1 N–K5[1]	N–K5	4 B–Q3[3]	N–B3
2 NxN	BxN	5 QxP[4]	
3 B–K1[2]	KR–B1		

[1] Very logical. Since Black's Knight defends QR2, White seeks to dislodge it. Now if 1 . . . NxN; 2 PxN, N–K5; 3 B–Q4 wins the QRP. (There is no need to play QxP immediately; better to preserve the two Bishops first.)

[2] White retains the two Bishops—Black is still saddled with the problem of how to defend his QRP. 3 QxP is a playable alternative, but White prefers first to tie his opponent into knots. Black now sacrifices his RP to obtain counterplay. 2 . . . R–R1 looks none too palatable.

[3] Threatening 5 RxB, RxR; 6 BxN.

[4] The rest is a matter of technique. White is a Pawn ahead.

Maintain access to backward Pawns

RESHEVSKY—D. BYRNE, ROSENWALD TOURNEY, NEW YORK, 1954–55

White moves. If a backward Pawn is on a closed file, then it is relatively difficult to gain access to it. When this same Pawn is exposed on an open file, it is altogether another matter. Black has just captured a White Knight on Q5. White now has the option of recapturing with either the Pawn or the Queen. Which choice is strategically correct?

Diagram 42

WHITE	BLACK	WHITE	BLACK
1 PxN?[1]	N–K2	3 P–B3	P–KN4
2 P–K4	P–B4	4 Q–Q3	O–O[2]

[1] This is a strategical error because it closes the Q-file. After 1 QxN! the question is whether Black can enforce P–Q4 in order to dissolve his backward QP. If not, he is positionally lost.

After 1 QxN, N–K2; 2 Q–Q2, P–Q4; 3 BxN!, KxB (forced— 3 . . . QxB; 4 PxP wins a clear Pawn for White); 4 QR–Q1, P–Q5 (4. . . PxP; 5 Q–N4ch wins Black's Queen); 5 PxP, PxP; 6 KR–K1 with a winning attack.

Passive defense is even worse: e.g., 1 QxN, B–B1; 2 QR–Q1, B–K2; 3 R–Q2 (pile on targets!), O–O; 4 KR–Q1, Q–B2; 5 N–B3, threatening N–K4, with a crushing bind.

[2] White has no time to profit from control of the open QB file because Black's K-side play must be counteracted. The game soon ended in a draw. After 6 QR–B1, PxP; 7 PxP, P–KR4; 8 RxRch, RxR; 9 R–KB1, RxR; 10 KxR, K–B2; 11 K–N2, K–N3; 12 P–R3, N–N1; 13 N–B3, N–B3; etc.

When possible, block access to backward Pawns

JACOBS—EVANS, U.S. OPEN CHAMPIONSHIP, 1955

Diagram 43

Black moves. When defending with a backward Pawn, your strategy should be to force your opponent to close his access to it. Often tactics provide the remedy.

Black has a glaring weakness on Q3. If he can force White to play N–Q5, so that, in the subsequent exchange, White will have to recapture with one of his Pawns rather than the Queen, then Black will have closed the Q-file and thus have solved his problem.

WHITE	BLACK	WHITE	BLACK
1 . . .	N–N3!	5 BxN	BxB
2 B–N3	B–N5[1]	6 N–Q5[3]	NxN
3 N–K1[2]	R–B1	7 KPxN	B–Q2[4]
4 Q–Q3	B–K3		

[1] A little finesse before returning to K3 with the Bishop. The threat of BxN develops a piece with gain of time.

[2] To prevent the doubling of the KB Pawns after BxN.

[3] Finally forced—it is the only way to defend the BP.

[4] Compare this position with the original one. Black has achieved his primary purpose: he has converted his QP into a bastion of strength. White has been forced to close the Q-file, and in the process Black has acquired the two Bishops. White has the bad Bishop. Finally, Black threatens to expand with P–KB4. White must now fight for the draw and, in fact, finally succumbed in another dozen moves.

When possible, repair backward Pawns

Backward Pawns provide natural targets and restrict freedom of movement. It stands to reason they should be dissolved (or "repaired") at every opportunity by any available means—tactical or otherwise. In the three positions that follow Black utilizes the move to repair his Pawn Structure.

FINKELSTEIN—EVANS,
MARSHALL CHESS CLUB CHAMPIONSHIP, 1946–47

Diagram 44

Correct is 1 . . . P–B4

Black takes advantage of the pin on the Bishop to advance his backward QBP. Moreover, this gains a tempo—White must delay castling owing to the threat of P–B5. Black has also opened a beautiful diagonal for his Q-Bishop (QR1–KR8).

Note that the tempting developing move 1 . . . B–K3 does not solve the problem of the backward QBP after White retreats with his Queen to B2. Then P–B4 could be met with the simple PxP.

Diagram 45

Correct is 1 . . . P–Q4

This time Black takes advantage of the indirect pin on White's KP:
2 NxP, NxN; 3 QxN, QxQ; 4 PxQ, BxN wins a piece. The best that
White now has is 2 B–Q3, whereupon either PxP or P–Q5 is satisfactory for Black.

Diagram 46

Correct is 1 . . . P–K4

Here there is not so much need for haste as in the previous two
positions. Black can even take time out to develop a piece with
1 . . . B–Q3 first, inasmuch as there is no way White can effectively
prevent P–K4. However, P–K4 must be played eventually, though
one might argue that the threat is stronger than the execution and
therefore it should be delayed for psychological reasons. The game

continued: **1 . . . P–K4; 2 PxP, N(2)xP; 3 B–B2, B–KN5; 4 P–KR3, BxN; 5 NxB, NxNch; 6 QxN, QxQ; 7 PxQ**—White has a very bad Pawn Structure and he lost the ensuing endgame.

The moral of it all is that as long as Pawns are mobile, they are healthy.

Doubled and Tripled Pawns

Diagram 47

Doubled Pawns

Doubled Pawns should be avoided because they cannot be mobilized. They frequently offer Space compensation, inasmuch as they provide an open file on which to operate.

Diagram 48

Tripled Pawns

Tripled Pawns represent the worst possible Pawn formation, with the single exception of quadrupled Pawns. They can be capped by only one enemy unit, as in the diagram, where one Black Pawn holds all three in place.

46

Immobile doubled Pawns

White moves. When doubled Pawns are "there to stay"—beware! All too often one of them can be picked off if your opponent simply focuses pieces on it. In this position White merely maneuvers his Knights to Q4 and K3. Even Black's two Bishops are of no avail.

Notice how Black would have a good game if only his Pawn were on KN2 instead of KB4.

Diagram 49

WHITE	BLACK	WHITE	BLACK
1 N–Q4	P–QB3[1]	3 O–O–O[2]	B–B4
2 N–K3	O–O	4 N(3)xP[3]	

[1] Equally hopeless is 1 . . . P–B4; 2 N–N5, K–Q2 (forced); 3 O–O–O, and the pin is fatal to Black.

[2] Adding insult to injury! The Pawn will not run away—White can capture it at his leisure—so he prefers to strengthen his position first by castling.

[3] White has won a Pawn. The rest is a matter of technique.

Double-edged doubled Pawns

HOROWITZ—EVANS, WERTHEIM MEMORIAL, NEW YORK, 1951

Black moves. Black has a genuine problem: whether to double White's QBP's by NxN or by BxN. Each move has its peculiar drawbacks and advantages. Which would you choose —and why?

Diagram 50

WHITE	BLACK	WHITE	BLACK
1 . . .	NxN[1]	7 Q–Q3[4]	N–K1
2 PxN	B–K2	8 P–B5	P–Q4
3 N–Q4	P–Q3[2]	9 P–QB4	P–QR3
4 R–Q1	Q–B2[3]	10 N–B3	P–Q5[5]
5 N–N5	Q–N1	11 N–R4	Q–B2
6 B–QR3	R–Q1	12 QR–N1	R–N1[6]

[1] Instead Black can give up the two Bishops—probably a wiser course—with 1 . . . BxN; 2 PxB, Q–R4; 3 B–N2—but it is not clear how Black can make headway against the doubled Pawns. If now 3 . . . N–Q3; 4 N–Q2, Q–B4; 5 Q–Q3—White holds everything and threatens to repulse the invader.

The next move loses a vital tempo. It gives White a Time–Space advantage to offset his bad Pawn Structure. How this conflict is resolved in the game is interesting.

[2] 3 . . . P–Q4 would be a good move—but inconsistent—since it would undo all Black's labors by allowing White to dissolve his doubled Pawns.

[3] A necessary evil. Black must submit to contortions because he is cramped. He would like first to play 4 . . . P–QR3, but 5 P–B5, P–Q4; 6 P–B6, P–QN4; but 7 P–QR4, opens all the lines.

[4] More accurate is 7 P–B5, PxP (disagreeably forced; not 7 . . . P–Q4; 8 P–B6!, BxB; 9 P–B7, winning the Queen!); 8 RxRch, BxR; 9 BxP, threatening the devastating B–Q6. In view of this possibility, it seems Black would have been better advised to select BxN as his first move. But these things are not always easy to foresee over-the-board.

[5] Black fights to see that White's Pawns stay doubled!

[6] Finally Black is out of danger. Now Q–B2 is threatened.

Capture toward the center

EVANS—J. CROSS, U.S. OPEN CHAMPIONSHIP, 1953

White moves. Often doubled Pawns are inevitable, as in this variation of the Sicilian Defense: 1 P–K4, P–QB4; 2 N–KB3, N–KB3; 3 P–K5, N–Q4; 4 N–B3, NxN. *The problem is whether White should recapture with his QP or his NP. In the first instance, he would free his Q-Bishop. Offhand, that would seem most desirable.*

Yet 5 NPxN is correct. Can you see why?

Diagram 51

WHITE	BLACK	WHITE	BLACK
5 NPxN[1]	P–Q4	7 P–Q4	PxP[2]
6 PxP ep.	QxP	8 PxP[3]	

[1] Despite the temptation to choose the line which offers more rapid development (5 QPxN), White must first consider his long-range prospects in Pawn Structure. Right now, it is true, Time is more important than anything else. But after Black catches up in Time all that he has to do is exchange his QP for White's KP in such a manner that his 3 Q-side Pawns will hold White's 4 Q-side Pawns at bay. The reasoning here is similar to Diagram 16, only in this case White does not obtain the two Bishops as compensation.

[2] Black should be more reluctant to exchange—he should play to keep White's Pawns doubled. After 7 . . . P–K3 however; 8 B–R3 exerts annoying pressure on Black's normal development.

[3] White has undoubled his Pawns and retains the initiative.

Immobile tripled Pawns

SMYSLOV—EVANS, HELSINKI OLYMPICS, 1952

Black moves. The reason tripled Pawns are bad, especially in the endgame, is that they cannot be mobilized. This is a drastic case. Black is a Pawn ahead, but it matters not. In effect the tripled Pawns count as one —and Black is in reality a Pawn down!

Diagram 52

WHITE	BLACK	WHITE	BLACK
1 . . .	P–B5[1]	4 K–Q6[3]	KxP
2 PxP	P–B4	5 K–K6	*Black Resigns*[4]
3 K–B6	P–B3[2]		

[1] Forced. If this Pawn could not advance, Black would be stalemated.

[2] Again forced. Not 3 . . . K–R2; 4 K–B7.

[3] Black was hoping for stalemate—but in vain—after 4 K–N6.

[4] White eats the Pawns at his leisure. A likely continuation might have been: 5 . . . K–B2; 6 KxP(4), K–Q2; 7 KxP, K–K1; 8 K–N5, etc.

Exchanges increase one's advantage in Pawn Structure

SMYSLOV—BOTVINNIK, 7TH MATCH GAME, 1954

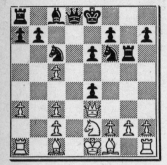

Diagram 53

Black moves. White is a Pawn ahead; albeit tripled, it exerts considerable pressure on Black's game. White's immediate threat is N–N3. Black utilizes a witty simplification which frees his game, exchanges Queens, and also leaves his King in its strongly centralized position for the ending.

WHITE	BLACK	WHITE	BLACK
1 ...	N–KN5	3 KxQ	NxPch
2 QxP	Q–Q8ch	4 K–K1	NxQ[1]

[1] Black's strategy has borne fruit in a hurry! Instead of exerting pressure, the tripled Pawns have suddenly been converted into positive endgame weaknesses, though White has compensation for his shattered Pawn Structure in the two Bishops. The chances are now roughly equal. The endgame ran an interesting course and White, in fact, finally won.

Just as each reduction of Force favors the side with superior Force, it also favors the side with the superior Pawn Structure. Pawn Structure becomes more important as the endgame nears because it is durable rather than transient in nature (like Time).

Weak squares

Diagram 54

A white square weakness

The sins of the weak player are revealed in his Pawn Structure.

A *"weak square complex"* is a series of similar colored squares which can never again be defended by Pawns because the Pawns (or Pawn) which normally defend them have already advanced. Remember—Pawns cannot retreat! This is the reason that unnecessary or prolific Pawn moves early in the game are ill-advised. Incidentally, a weak square complex is even weaker when the Bishop that would normally nurse it has been exchanged.

A *"hole"* is a square which can never again be defended by a Pawn. In the above diagram, Q3 and K4 are both holes for white.

"Weak squares" are characterized by a sense of emptiness. They need not be any particular color. *When Pawns are placed on black, the white squares are weak; when placed on white, the dark squares are weak.*

Whenever a Pawn advances, a fresh weakness is incurred. Naturally, this does not mean that Pawn moves should altogether be avoided. But it means that they should be made sparingly, either to free the pieces or with some other definite objective in mind.

Diagram 55

Weak "Luft" and strong "Luft"

In making "Luft," one is generally confronted with the choice of pushing either the RP or the NP. (If you are unfamiliar with "Luft," consult Diagram 120). The RP is advisable because it does not create any holes.

In the above diagram Black's formation involves two holes (at his QR3 and QB3). White has created no holes. The slight weakening of the KN3 square is offset by the presence of the KBP. Therefore his configuration is more desirable.

Avoid needless weaknesses

EVANS—KRAUSS, OFFHAND GAME, NEW YORK, 1945

Diagram 56

Black moves. *This message can never be repeated too often. If the beginner does not know what to do, he generally pushes the nearest piece of wood and, since the Pawns are most numerous, this unlucky selection all too often falls on them.*

White has just played a horrible move—P–KN3. Why is this bad—and what move would have been better?

The correct move would have been **B–Q3,** developing a piece and preparing to castle. Instead, White has irreparably weakened his white squares by preparing to place his Bishop where it can serve no good function: KN2. The fianchetto is not good here because the Bishop would have no scope. In the words of Nimzovitch, it would "bite on granite." The "granite" refers to Black's solid Pawn mass: Q4, K3, QB3. The K's fianchetto is a good formation in these close openings only if there is a possibility that lines will be opened for it in the ensuing action. Pieces should be developed in active not passive positions.

Occupy holes

EVANS—JOYNER, U.S. JUNIOR CHAMPIONSHIP, 1949

Diagram 57

White moves. Black has a gaping hole on his QB3. If it were his move, he could partially repair it with . . . BxN followed by . . . P–QB4. On principle White ought to occupy this hole with **1 N–B6.** *Here, by accident, this move also happens to win by force.*

WHITE	BLACK	WHITE	BLACK
1 N–B6	Q–B3[1]	3 BxP!	KR–K1[2]
2 BxB	QxB	4 B–B3[3]	

[1] If 1 . . . BxN; 2 BxB, PxB; 3 QxB wins at least a Pawn without allowing Black any counterplay.
[2] Not 3 . . . QxB?; 4 N–K7ch.
[3] White has won a Pawn and the rest is technique. If now 4 . . . BxN; 5 BxB, QR–Q1; 6 P–K4, etc.

Exploit holes

Black moves. *White has two gaping holes: KR4 and KB4. Black already occupies one with the Rook. The problem is to occupy the other. So Black must ask himself what piece he wants there. The last problem is how to get it there.*
The answer is **1 . . . N–B1!**
Why?

Diagram 58

WHITE	BLACK	WHITE	BLACK
1 . . .	N–B1[1]	6 Q–K3	R–R1
2 R–QR1	N–N3	7 R–QB1	RxR
3 B–B1[2]	R–B6[3]	8 QxR	QxQ
4 R–Q3	Q–B2	9 BxQ	NxP[4]
5 BxP	RxBP		

[1] The idea is to swing the Knight to N3 and thence to KB5.

[2] The hapless Bishop cannot do everything at once! Now White can invade on the hole which has just been created on QB3.

[3] Here, again, Black follows the principle of occupying holes.

[4] Black has won a Pawn with an easy victory to follow. Pawn Structure has finally been converted into superior Force. Notice that here, as so often, it is the *theme*, the *threat*, of a given plan that forces the win—even though that plan may never literally be carried out. The need to prevent Black's Knight from reaching his KB4 forced White to leave his other weakness (on QB3) unguarded.

Force entry to weak squares

EVANS (U.S.A.)—KESTEN (FRANCE), DUBROVNIK OLYMPICS, 1950

Diagram 59

White moves. By all standards Black's Q3 is a weak square; i.e., there is no Pawn which can guard it. What White must do is to utilize the pin on the KP in order to bring his Knight from its passive position on KN3 to an active one at Q6. This is a good example of converting Time into Space (made possible by an opponent's weak square complex).

WHITE	BLACK	WHITE	BLACK
1 N–B5	Q–QB2	3 PxP	N–Q4
2 P–K5[1]	PxP	4 N–Q6[2]	

[1] The weakness of a square must often be evaluated in terms of what attacking pieces can practically be brought to bear on it. This advance secures White control of his Q6. It does cede Black the square Q4 for his Knight (every advance creates a new weakness), but this is no time to be niggardly! In chess, as in advertising, it pays to give a little in order to get a lot. Black's Knight can always be dislodged by the simple expedient of BxN (after it gets to Q4), whereas White's Knight on Q6 stands like a house.

[2] This final position is the culmination of a spatial combination. White has the initiative and Black is cramped. Note that if Black had had a sound Pawn Structure to begin with (Pawn on KB2 instead of on KB3) there would have been no way for White to exploit the hole on Q6.

The remaining moves were: 4 . . . R–K2; 5 N–Q4, P–QR3; 6 B–N3, P–B4; 7 NxKP, NxN; 8 NxB, N(4)–B5; 9 N–Q6 (home again!), K–R1; 10 P–N3, N–N3; 11 Q–K4, R–KB1; 12 P–B4, N–Q5; 13 B–Q5, Q–Q2; 14 QR–K1, N–N4; 15 N–B7ch, R(1)xN; 16 BxR, Q–Q5ch; 17 QxQ, NxQ; 18 P–K6, R–B2; 19 BxN, Black Resigns.

Invade weak squares

White moves. Black's advantages are manifold: his King is active, his pieces are centralized, and White has weak squares on Q3 and K3. (Note the characteristic "emptiness" around these squares.)

The problem for Black is how to penetrate on the K-file. This is solved instructively in the game.

Diagram 60

WHITE	BLACK	WHITE	BLACK
1 BxB[1]	NxB	7 N–Q4	RxP
2 KR–K1	N–B7	8 RxR	NxR
3 RxR	RxR	9 NxP	N–Q8
4 R–Q1	R–K7[2]	10 P–QB4	K–B3
5 P–N3	N–K6	11 N–Q4	K–K4[3]
6 R–QN1	N–B5		

[1] The King and Pawn ending would be drawn *if* White could only get to it. Exchanges would help White—but he can't exchange enough pieces. Black needs only a Rook and a Knight in order to carry out a successful invasion. If White's Pawn were on KB2 and QB2 (instead of KB3 and QB3), he would be all right.

[2] Finally penetrating! The Knight is immune because of mate on the last rank. White now makes "Luft" for his King, but this involves the creation of new weaknesses.

[3] Black has a winning position—he penetrates on White's weak black squares. This is more than a gratuitous assertion, as will be seen from the instructive course of the game: 12 N–N3, P–QN3; 13 K–N1, P–B4; 14 K–B1, N–K6ch; 15 K–K2, NxP (that old black magic finally hits pay dirt!); 16 K–Q3, K–Q4; 17 P–B4, P–QN4; 18 P–N4, P–N5; 19 N–B1, P–QR4; 20 N–K2, P–R5; 21 N–N3, P–R6; 22 N–K2, N–Q3; 23 N–B1, N–K5; 24 K–K3, P–B5; 25 P–R4, N–B4; 26 N–K2, N–K5; 27 N–B1, N–B6; 28 P–R5, NxP; 29 NxN, P–N6; 30 N–B3ch, K–K3; 31 P–B5ch, K–B2; 32 K–Q4, P–R7; 33 KxP, P–N8(Q); White Resigns.

Every Pawn advance creates a fresh weakness

KAUFMAN—EVANS, U.S. OPEN CHAMPIONSHIP, 1955

White moves. This concept is so highly theoretical that it is comforting to find an example in practical play—even if one does happen to be on the wrong end of it!

Black has just played P–KR3, "putting the question" to the Bishop. White's reply comes as a rude shock!

Diagram 61

WHITE	BLACK	WHITE	BLACK
1 BxP!	**PxB**	**2 Q–K3**	**K–N2[1]**

[1]This move gives White his piece back without a fight.
The alternatives are: e.g.,

  I. 1 . . . B–Q3; 2 QxKRP, R–K1; 3 RxRch, NxR (if 3 . . . QxR; 4 QxN); 4 B–R7ch, K–R1; 5 B–N6 dis. ch, K–N1; 6 Q–R7ch, K–B1; 7 QxP mate.

 II. 1 . . . B–K3; 2 QxKRP, R–K1; 3 R–K3 and wins.

III. 1 . . . R–K1; 2 QxKRP, B–B1; 3 RxR and wins. (If 3 . . . QxR; 4 QxN. And on 3 . . . NxR comes 4 Q–R7, mate.)

IV. 1 . . . N–K5; 2 NxN, PxN; 3 QxKP with the double threat of Q–R7 mate and/or QxB.

 V. 1 . . . P–Q5! 2 QxRP, Q–Q3! 3 Q–N5 ch, K–R1; 4 RxB, QxR; and White seems to have no more than a perpetual. On 5 N–K4!? N–N1! holds.

The game actually continued with **3 QxB, QxQ; 4 RxQ,** and White won a Pawn. Though Black succeeded in drawing the endgame, he should have lost.

58

Pawn chains

Diagram 62

A healthy Pawn chain

A healthy Pawn chain is one which has its base either on or as near to its original square as possible. In the diagram, the base of White's Pawn at K5 is on QN2. Pawn chains, to be undermined, must be attacked at their base. Hence it stands to reason that the further this base is removed from enemy forces the harder it is to get at.

Diagram 63

A diseased Pawn chain

This Pawn position is slightly diseased. Note that the Pawn on K5 has only two links (Q4 and QB3) compared to three links in the previous diagram.

A "*chain*" is thus a series of connected Pawns which have reached a point at which the one furthest advanced is organically linked to the one which is least advanced. Pawn chains are as strong as their weakest link.

Even when a Pawn chain is healthy, it involves a weak square complex. In both diagrams White is weak on his white squares (Q3, K4, Q5).

59

Avoid diseased Pawn chains

MENGARINI—EVANS, U.S. CHAMPIONSHIP, 1951

White moves. Diseased Pawn Structures are characterized by advanced bases and lack of mobility. Even opposite colored Bishops do not help White. White's Pawns are so far advanced that they can be had for the mere picking. Contrast them with Black's healthy K-side Pawns which have a sound base on KB2.

Diagram 64

WHITE	BLACK	WHITE	BLACK
1 K–K1[1]	KxP	7 K–B1	B–N5[3]
2 B–Q4	K–K5[2]	8 K–Q2	B–K3
3 B–B3	K–K6	9 K–B1	B–N6
4 K–Q1	B–N5ch	10 K–Q2	B–B7
5 K–B1	K–K5	11 K–B1	K–B5
6 K–Q2	B–K7	12 B–Q4	K–N6[4]

[1] White is in "Zugzwang," meaning the unpleasant obligation to move. If 1 B–K3, K–N6; 2 K–K1, KxP; 3 K–B2, K–N5 wins. Or, even simpler, after 1 B–K3 is B–K5 and White must lose his BP due to "Zugzwang."

[2] Triangulation. 2 . . . K–N6 would only be met by B–B2ch.

[3] There is no rush. Black prefers to strengthen his position before going after the RP.

[4] Black now has an easy win. All that he has to do is advance his RP.

Challenge advanced Pawn bases

Diagram 65

Black moves. It has already been determined that a Pawn chain is strongest when its base stands on the original second rank. Each time this base is advanced, the chain is weakened. It is even good strategy sometimes to bait the center forwards. Black has just played P–QN3, provoking White's reply P–QN4. Now— with one stroke—Black can reduce White's Q-side Pawn Structure to a shambles. How?

WHITE	BLACK	WHITE	BLACK
1 ...	P–QR4!	5 R–K1	PxP
2 B=Q2[1]	PxNP	6 BxP	BxB
3 BxP	N–R3	7 PxB	Q–B2
4 BxN	BxB	8 Q–B2	KR–B1[2]

[1] White has no satisfactory reply:
  I. If 2 P–N5, PxP; 3 PxP, BxP wins a Pawn.
 II. If 2 PxNP, PxP wins a Pawn.
III. If 2 P–QR3, PxNP wins a Pawn because of the pin on the R-file. Note that if Black did not play 1 . . . P–QR4 immediately, then White would have had time for B–N2 so as to meet P–QR4 with P–QR3.

[2] White's Q-side structure is shattered. White is saddled with a weak isolated Pawn under constant fire.

Strike Pawn chains at their base

ADAMS—EVANS, NEW YORK METROPOLITAN LEAGUE, 1951

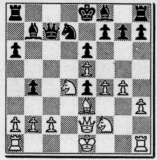

Diagram 66

Black moves. The base of White's Pawn on K5 is the Pawn on KB4. Black must find some way to strike at the base.

It's as simple as pricking a balloon with a pin—everything explodes.

WHITE	BLACK	WHITE	BLACK
1 . . .	P–N4![1]	5 O–O–O	N–N3
2 P–B5[2]	QxP	6 PxP	N–Q4
3 PxP	PxP	7 R–R6	O–O[3]
4 P–KR4	B–B4	8 RxKP	QxR
	Black Resigns[4]		

[1] Black literally smashes up his own K-side in order to destroy White's Pawn chain. Is it worth it? It is a question of evaluation. In the endgame, of course, such a move would be played only after the most extreme deliberation. But this is not the endgame. It is the middle-game. Black reckons that his influence in the center is more important *right now* than Pawn Structure.

[2] The best chance. 2 PxP, QxP gives Black a beautifully centralized game while all White's pieces remain cluttered in an awkward quasi-blockade. Incidentally, 2 O–O–O is out of the question because of PxP; 3 BxP, P–K6 winning the exchange.

[3] This looks anti-positional, but Black sees a quick win. This is no longer a question of strategy—but of tactics. Ordinarily one should never castle into such an exposed position.

[4] After 9 NxQ, BxBch; 10 K–N1, RxN; 11 Q-any, R–QB1 White's Queen is no match for the minor pieces.

Notice how quickly White's game fell apart as soon as his center collapsed.

Try to weaken strong bases

EVANS—DAKE, U.S. OPEN CHAMPIONSHIP, 1955

Diagram 67

White moves. Black's position seems very sound. Upon closer examination, however, we see that the dark squares on his K-side (KR3, KB3) are weak. All Black's pieces, moreover, are clustered on the Q-wing. Thus this seems like a propitious moment to storm Black's fortress. In order to do this White must invade at KN6. Before he can invade, the base Pawn (at KB2) must be undermined.

WHITE	BLACK	WHITE	BLACK
1 P–B5[1]	N(3)–Q2[2]	5 N–N4	N(4)–Q2
2 P–K6	N–B1	6 B–Q4ch	K–B2
3 PxPch	KxP	7 R–K1[4]	
4 N–K5ch[3]	K–N2		

[1] With the devastating threat of P–K6.

[2] An attempt to bring the Knight which is out-of-play to the aid of the embattled monarch. It is extraordinary that Black is already without any satisfactory defense. If 1 . . . R–Q1; 2 RxRch, BxR; 3 P–K6!, PxKP; 4 PxNP leaves Black's Pawn Structure a shambles. 1 . . . PxP; 2 QxP, N–K3 (to prevent R–Q4); 3 N–K4 leads to a winning attack against Black's exposed King.

[3] It is incredible how quickly Black's position falls apart now that his base Pawn has been destroyed.

[4] There is now no good defense against N–R6ch followed by P–B6. Note that in the original diagram even if Black's Pawn were on KN2, White would still have a strong attack with P–B5. Had Black's Pawn Structure been intact, it would have merely been harder to make headway.

Expose enemy bases

EVANS—ADAMS, LOG CABIN CHESS CLUB CHAMPIONSHIP, 1950

Diagram 68

White moves. White's chain extends from QB2 to KB5. If it were Black's move, 1 . . . P–B5 would undermine the entire chain by shifting the base from B2 to Q3 after the consequent exchange of Pawns. If White takes time to move his Queen out of the pin (to prevent P–B5), then Black would have time for P–KB3, consolidating his chain from KN2 to K4.

WHITE	BLACK	WHITE	BLACK
1 P–B6![1]	PxP	15 P–KR4	P–B4[8]
2 N–N3![2]	P–B5![3]	16 P–R5	K–Q2[9]
3 QR–Q1	PxP	17 R–R7ch	K–Q3
4 PxP	N–Q5	18 P–R6	P–B5
5 Q–KB2	P–KB4	19 R–R8	RxKP
6 BxN![4]	QxB	20 P–R7	RxPch
7 QxQ	RxQ	21 K–B2	R–R5
8 NxP	NxN	22 R–Q8ch	K–B4
9 RxN[5]	KR–Q1	23 P–R8(Q)	RxQ
10 RxBP	RxQP	24 RxR	K–Q5
11 RxR	RxR	25 K–K2	K–B6
12 R–B6	R–Q7[6]	26 R–R8	P–N4
13 RxP	RxP	27 RxP	P–N5
14 P–N4!	R–K7[7]	28 R–QB7	*Black Resigns*[10]

[1] This Pawn is used as a battering ram in order to force Black to double his Pawns, thus exposing the base of the KP on an open file (at KB3). The sacrifice of a Pawn is only temporary, and the voluntary opening of the KN file on White's castled King is not dangerous because there is no way Black can make use of it for an attack. This game is instructive because it emphasizes the long-term importance of destroying Pawn chains, even at the short-term cost of a Pawn.

[2] White must continue sharply. 2 Q–K1 would be met by P–B4! returning the Pawn under favorable circumstances: e.g., 3 PxP, P–B3! and all is well again—Black has managed to close the KB-file. 2 BxRP, instead of the text, would be met handily by P–B5.

[3] Black counterattacks—rather than maintain the role of passive defender. The principle behind his play is that an attack on the wing is best met by a reaction in the center.

[4] Thematic. White must never play PxP, but capture in such a manner that he keeps the KB-file open.

[5] Note that both sides now have exposed bases: White's Pawn on Q3 and Black's Pawn on KB2. Black is lost because White comes first in the element of Time. The remainder of the game shows why.

[6] 12 . . . R–Q8ch; 13 K–B2, R–Q7ch; 14 K–B3, RxQNP gains a tempo but puts White's King in a more favorable position. Still, it might have been preferable. Time is now more important than anything else. It is essential to get the passed Pawns moving! Incidentally, after 12 . . . R–Q3; 13 RxR, PxR; 14 K–B2, K–Q2; 15 K–B3, K–K3; 16 P–KN4, P–Q4; 17 PxPch, KxP; 18 P–KR4 White wins by virtue of that old weevil, the outside pass pawn.

[7] Black cannot stop for 14 RxQRP because the White Pawns are too fast after 15 P–N5. The important thing is mobility, not material. Black must try to mobilize his Q-side Pawns as quickly as possible. He cannot stop to defend himself or feast on Pawns.

[8] Too slow, but there is hardly anything better. 15 . . . RxKP; 16 R–N6, P–B4; 17 P–R5 also wins for White.

[9] Not the tempting 16 . . . P–B5 because of 17 R–B6ch followed by RxBP.

[10] A really beautiful and instructive game—more or less forced from the original diagram. White converted Time (the fact that it was originally his move) into better Pawn Structure, at the cost of Force (1 P–B6!). His better Pawn Structure, however, was later re-converted into superior Force when Black was forced to sacrifice his Rook to prevent the RP from queening. A game of chess is an organic whole.

From the diagram it is immediately apparent that a good Bishop commands mobility and open lines, whereas a bad Bishop is hemmed in by its own Pawns, thus serving a purely defensive role. There is no theology in chess. When a Bishop is bad it is not wicked, just useless. It is generally good policy to place Pawns on a color opposite that of the Bishop, as Black has done in the diagram. When this is impossible, try to get rid of the Bishop. Pawn Structure intimately affects the working value of the pieces. The Bishops work best on an open board. Conversely, with two Knights against two Bishops, one would attempt to lock the Pawn formation. Knights are superior to Bishops in closed positions because they can leap over obstacles and barricades.

Note one other thing in the diagram: White has no piece with which to attack Black's Pawn on QN4, whereas his Bishop is tied down to the defense of his own QNP.

White has the bad Bishop;
Black has the good Bishop

White has the good Knight;
Black has the bad Bishop

Diagram 69

Diagram 70

HALPER—EVANS, MARSHALL CHESS CLUB CHAMPIONSHIP, 1948–49

White has the good Knight; Black has the bad Bishop

White has a stranglehold on the dark squares. His Knight irradiates sunshine. Contrast this with Black's sour Bishop which "bites on granite." Black has no counterplay. He is helpless against the threatened R–QR3 followed by RxP and the eventual advance of the QRP. A drastic example of paralysis—known in chess jargon as a "bind." Rather than wait for the coffin to arrive, Black resigned in this position.

The good Knight against the bad Bishop

GOMPERT—EVANS,
MARSHALL CHESS CLUB JUNIOR CHAMPIONSHIP, 1946

Diagram 71

White moves. Black wins. White's Bishop seems to command open lines, yet it has nothing to strike at. White's Pawns, moreover, are on the same color as his Bishop. White has no piece with which to defend his white squares and thus cannot prevent Black from invading.

Contrast Black's beautifully centralized Knight with White's ineffectual Bishop. This is not quite so cut-and-dried as the previous example.

WHITE	BLACK	WHITE	BLACK
1 R–Q3[1]	RxP	3 K–N2	RxP[3]
2 R–Q2[2]	R–N6ch		

[1] White is desperate. The threat was 1 . . . R–KR7 followed by R(1)–K7. White tries to bring this Rook into play at the cost of a Pawn. 1 R–Q1 holds out longer. Then 1 . . . R–R7; 2 R–Q2, R–R8 forces penetration.

[2] To prevent 2 . . . R(1)–K7.

[3] Black's two extra Pawns assure him of an easy win. Note the passive role played by White's Bishop throughout the preceding action.

The Queen side majority

Diagram 72

Black has a potential outside passed Pawn. The Q-side
majority, characterized by an unbalanced Pawn Structure, generally
leads to a sharp game because the themes are so forcibly outlined.
White must try to use his "qualitative majority" in the center (with
P–K4 and P–Q5—this would be known as the "inside passed Pawn"
in the endgame), whereas Black must try to cash in on his distant
majority. The Q-side majority is an endgame advantage because it
promises a potential outside passed Pawn. Of course, this is true
only when both sides have castled K-side, which is usually the case.
Black's King holds White's K-side majority at bay, whereas White's
King must scurry to the Q-side to prevent the passed Pawn from
queening. (See Diagram 15 for the principle involved.)

Cash in on a Q-side majority

EVANS—POMAR, U.S. OPEN CHAMPIONSHIP, 1954

White moves. White has a Q-side majority (2 *against* 1 *on the Queen side). Black has the inside passed Pawn (the QBP).*
White's problem is to demolish the blockade and to mobilize his potential passed Pawn.

Diagram 73

WHITE	BLACK	WHITE	BLACK
1 P–N6![1]	PxP[2]	6 R–R6ch	K–B4
2 P–R7	R–QR1	7 K–K3	P–B7
3 R–QN2	P–B5[3]	8 K–Q2[4]	P–B4
4 RxNP	P–B6	9 NPxP	PxP
5 R–N7ch	K–Q3	10 R–N8[5]	

[1] A temporary sacrifice of a Pawn in order to get the RP moving.
[2] Forced. 2 . . . P–B5 loses to 3 P–N7, R–QN1; 4 RxP, followed by R–B8.
[3] A desperate attempt to achieve some counterplay.
[4] Notice how easily White's King stops this Pawn, whereas Black's King cannot cross to the scene of action.
[5] White wins a full Rook.

69

Mobilize a Q-side majority

EVANS—KALME, HOLLYWOOD OPEN, 1954

Diagram 74

White moves. For the moment White is apparently stymied on the Q-wing. 1 P–N5 seems to lose a Pawn. Not so. Tactics provide the answer. Notice how, in the sequence, Black's proud, protected QP becomes transformed into a scraggly "isolani."

WHITE	BLACK	WHITE	BLACK
1 P–N5![1]	PxP[2]	8 R–K1	K–B2
2 P–B6[3]	Q–Q1	9 Q–N7	Q–Q3
3 PxP	BxN[4]	10 RxB!	QxR
4 QxB	NxP	11 BxP	QxB
5 Q–N2	N–B2	12 QxR	N–K3
6 B–R6[5]	P–B3	13 P–B7	N–N4
7 BxR	QxB	14 Q–K8ch	*Black Resigns*

[1] The blockade at QB3 must be demolished!

[2] No better is 1 . . . BxN; 2 QxB, PxP; 3 B–R6, winning the exchange.

[3] Equally good is 2 PxP, and if NxP; 3 P–B6. However, Black has the resource 2 . . . BxN. This, too, can be met by 3 P–B6, BxB; 4 PxQ, BxQ; 5 PxR(Q), RxQ; 6 RxB, winning the exchange. The text is more accurate because it narrows down Black's possible replies.

[4] Otherwise White's Pawn mass would soon become devastating.

[5] White wins the exchange. It is amazing how quickly Black's game now falls apart.

The minority attack

EVANS—OPSAHL, DUBROVNIK OLYMPICS, 1950

Black moves. The consequences of permitting an opponent's Q-side majority to mobilize have already become apparent. Here White has taken active measures to immobilize Black's majority by inaugurating a "minority attack," i.e., his two Q-side Pawns have been used as battering rams. The net aim of this strategy is to convert Black's potential strength into weakness instead.

Diagram 75

WHITE	BLACK	WHITE	BLACK
1 . . .	RPxP	3 P–N3	QR–K1
2 PxP	B–R6	4 PxP	PxP

19 moves later. White moves. Black now has a backward QBP. Nineteen moves later, after some of the pieces had been exchanged, the game continued from this position.

Diagram 76

WHITE	BLACK	WHITE	BLACK
1 N–B5ch[1]	K–B3	6 R–N7	P–B3
2 N–Q7ch	K–K3	7 N–R7	K–K3[5]
3 N–B8ch	K–B3[2]	8 N–B8ch	K–B2
4 N–R7ch	K–K3	9 NxP[6]	KxN
5 N–N5ch[3]	K–Q3[4]	10 RxN[7]	K–B4

71

WHITE	BLACK	WHITE	BLACK
11 R–QB7	R–QB8	26 K–N3	K–N4
12 R–QB8	K–N3	27 R–R4	K–B4
13 K–N3	R–B7	28 R–B4ch	K–N4
14 P–R4	K–B4	29 R–N4ch	K–B4[9]
15 R–KR8	K–N3	30 K–R4	R–R1
16 P–B5ch	KxP	31 R–N7	R–R1
17 RxPch	K–N3[8]	32 P–R6	R–R8
18 R–R8	K–B4	33 R–N3	R–R8ch
19 R–KN8	R–B8	34 R–R3	R–KN8
20 K–N2	R–QR8	35 R–B3ch![10]	K–N3
21 P–R5	R–R2	36 R–N3ch	RxR
22 R–N3	R–R2	37 KxR	KxP
23 R–R3	K–N4	38 K–N4	K–N3
24 K–B3	R–R3	39 K–B4	K–N2
25 R–R1	K–B4	40 K–B5	K–B2
		41 P–B3	*Black Resigns*[11]

[1] Black's Knight is tied to the defense of the neurotic QBP. White now wins a Pawn by a curious Knight's tour.

[2] Always forced. Not 3 . . . K–Q3??; 4 R–Q7 mate.

[3] Completing the amazing arc!

[4] No better is 5 . . . K–B3; 6 P–B3! followed by the steamroller—P–K4–5.

[5] Not 7 . . . P–B4?; 8 N–B8 and the threat of mate on Q7 will cost Black dearly.

[6] Finally the pin pays dividends.

[7] Now that White has won a Pawn the rest is a matter of technique. The remaining moves are extremely instructive, and they are given here in their entirety for those who are interested in perfecting their Rook and Pawn endings.

[8] White's extra, doubled Pawn has been converted into an extra, passed Pawn.

[9] 29 . . . KxP loses to 30 R–R4ch, K–N4; 31 RxR, KxR; 32 K–N4, K–N3; 33 K–B4. This happens later.

[10] Not 35 P–R7, R–N5ch—Black gets a perpetual check!

[11] White has the opposition and this is decisive. If 41 . . . K–K2; 42 K–N6, K–K3; 43 P–B4, P–B4 (or 43 . . . K–K2; 44 P–B5); 44 K–N5, winning a Pawn. The same is true if Black moves his King to the other side: 41 . . . K–N2; 42 K–K6, K–N3; 43 P–B4, etc.

CHAPTER THREE: Force

Force is the fist of the chessboard. And in a purely physical struggle, the stronger is bound to win. So it is with chess: "when right opposes right, force decides"—or might makes right! If victory is the goal of the game, then the accumulation of force is the chief means to that end. Of all the elements force is the most important and in itself comes closest to being the most decisive. Generally a big advantage in the other elements culminates in, or must first be converted into Force, before it becomes sufficient to win. Reuben Fine expressed this with the quip, "I would rather have a Pawn than a finger!"

The basic principle of Force is that *material superiority is decisive when all other things are equal.** In fact, a test of one's technical skill is how easily one can convert Force into victory. (Technique can be acquired only by constant practice and study of master games. This book takes technique for granted, and no attempt is made to teach it here.)

In practice, of course, "other things" generally are not "equal." There are always little obstacles to be surmounted, it seems, just when things are brightest. One side may be a Pawn ahead in an endgame, yet not win because of opposite colored Bishops—or stalemate. In a gambit, one side may be a Knight ahead yet decisively behind in Time and Space. It then becomes a matter of weighing an advantage in one element against a disadvantage in another, of balancing, of compensating. This is essentially a problem in evaluation (see Chapter 7).

The following table expresses the importance of the pieces in relation to each other with one unit taken as the smallest measure of strength:

TABLE OF RELATIVE VALUES

Pieces	Relative Values
Pawn	1 unit
Knight	$3\frac{1}{2}$ units
Bishop	$3\frac{1}{2}$ units
Rook	5 units
Queen	10 units

Another way of expressing it is in terms of money: the Pawn is

---

* Of course there are exceptions—such as two Knights being unable to effect mate against a lone King.

worth 10 cents, Knights and Bishops 35 cents apiece, the Rooks fifty cents, and the Queen one dollar. The King has no fixed value. In the opening, where it must find shelter and take no active part in the proceedings, it is worth about twenty cents. In the endgame, however, where it may wander freely, generally without any fear of mate, it becomes a valuable attacking piece and is worth about forty cents.

The important thing to remember is that this table expresses abstract relationships under so-called "ideal" conditions, and that the value of pieces change as positions change. Sometimes a well-placed Knight may be worth more than a Rook, whereas a Pawn on the seventh rank which cannot be stopped from queening is obviously worth infinitely more than the same Pawn under ordinary circumstances.

Superior force confers the same advantage as starting a poker game with more chips. You can keep crowding your near-bankrupt opponent with bigger bets on each hand.

The smallest unit of force is the Pawn. In the following position "other things are equal"—so superior Force wins!

Diagram 77

White wins whoever moves. *The win is elementary. White must only be careful that he does not permit Black's King to get in front of the Pawn. Thus, if* **1 . . . K–Q4; 2 K–B5!** (*not 2 P–K4ch, K–K3–draw*), **K–Q3; 3 P–K4, K–K2; 4 K–K5, K–Q2** (*Black's King cannot stay in front of the Pawn because White has the opposition. Black's King is forced to one side or the other—he has free will to the extent that he can choose his own method of dying*); **5 K–B6, K–K1; 6 K–K6!, K–Q1; 7 K–B7, K–Q2; 8 P–K5** *and the Pawn is chaperoned in to the queening square. Of course, if White has the first move, it is much simpler because P–K4 would win immediately.*

74

The General Pattern for Converting Force into Victory

Once having won material, the general pattern is to keep exchanging pieces and steering for the endgame. We have seen that even the lowly Pawn acquires Herculean properties in the ending.

Diagram 78

White wins by exchanging all the pieces. *White wins easily after* **1 RxR, RxR; 2 RxR, KxR; 3 K–K2**—*followed by centralizing his King and advancing the QRP. Conversely, if it were Black's move instead, his best chance to draw would consist in preserving at least one Rook after* **1 . . . RxR; 2 RxR, R–QR1.**

The Two Bishops

In theory a Knight is equal to a Bishop (they each tally $3\frac{1}{2}$ units in the table of relative values). In practice a Bishop is preferable to a Knight (especially in open positions and the endgame where it can sweep the board). Two Bishops against two Knights constitute an advantage in Space rather than Force—and woe unto him who exchanges Bishop for Knight without just cause! The Knight has a more limited range than the Bishop. For this reason Bishops working in unison gain in strength as the endgame approaches. Therefore, if you find yourself with Bishop and Knight against two Bishops, make an attempt to exchange one of your opponent's Bishops. The exception is when the Pawn Structure is so locked that the Bishops have become a liability because their range has been seriously impaired. It is, however, much easier to open a game at will than to close it. The player with the two Bishops always stands ready to profit from the consequent opening of lines.

Play to "win" the two Bishops

EVANS—FINE, SEXTANGULAR MASTERS', NEW YORK, 1951

Diagram 79

Black moves. The two Bishops constitute a powerful weapon—but they are not inherited; an active effort must be made to "win" them in the middle game.

If a Knight is also worth $3\frac{1}{2}$ units, one may well be justified in demanding to know why all this fuss about the "two Bishops." The truth is, a Bishop is actually worth about $3\frac{3}{4}$ units—this is what a century of chess theory has taught us!

WHITE	BLACK	WHITE	BLACK
1 . . .	N–B5![1]	3 NxN	Q–R4
2 Q–B2[2]	NxB	4 B–Q2[3]	QxP[4]

[1] Also good is 1 . . . N(4)–N5; 2 QxQ, RxQ; 3 P–QR3, NxP!; 4 QN–Q2 (if 4 PxN, N–N6 regains the piece most favorably), N–B3. In this variation Black retains only a slight advantage. The text not only recaptures the Pawn—but wins the two Bishops in the process.

[2] Not 2 QxQ, NxPch; 3 K–R1, RxQ and White must lose at least a Pawn owing to the double threat of NxB or NxP. (4 B–K3 leaves the QNP hanging.)

[3] White should not attempt to hold onto the Pawn with 4 B–K3, B–B4; 5 Q–B1, QR–B1—Black regains the Pawn and his pieces spring into dynamic play.

[4] Black regains the Pawn with the better game. Play continued: 5 QxQ, NxQ; 6 B–B3, P–K4 (exchanging would lose the two Bishops); 7 B–N4, P–N3; 8 N–B3 and White managed to equalize.

Two Bishops against two Knights

BISGUIER—KASHDAN, HOLLYWOOD OPEN, 1954

White moves. Two Bishops working in unison sweep the board when the lines are open. The winning process consists of (1) hemming in the enemy Knights with Pawns, (2) tying them down to the defense of a weakness, (3) making inroads with the King, (4) liquidating pieces at a favorable moment. This ideal formula arises more frequently than one would imagine. This is a good case in point.

Diagram 80

WHITE	BLACK	WHITE	BLACK
1 P–QN4	PxP	5 BxN	NxB
2 PxP[1]	N–K3[2]	6 BxP	P–B4ch[6]
3 B–R4[3]	N(3)–B1[4]	7 K–B4	P–R3
4 K–K4	K–Q3[5]	8 B–Q4[7]	

[1] Driving Black's Knight back and completing the hemming in process.

[2] On 2 . . . N–R3; 3 B–B3 followed by K–Q4, also squeezes Black to death.

[3] Threatening 4 BxN. Notice that Black's Knight is tied down to the defense on the weak QNP.

[4] The exchange does not help Black. E.g., 3 . . . NxB; 4 KxN, N–B3; 5 P–B5, PxP; 6 KxP—the outside, passed QNP is decisive.

[5] To prevent K–Q5 and K–B6.

[6] Equally hopeless is 6 . . . NxB; 7 P–B5ch, K–B3; 8 PxN, KxP; 9 K–K5 and Black's K-side Pawns become easy prey.

[7] The Black Pawns must fall. White has converted his spatial advantage into Force.

Two Bishops against Bishop and Knight

BURGER—EVANS, U.S. OPEN CHAMPIONSHIP, 1952

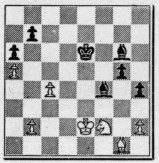

Black moves. *As a team the two Bishops are powerful because, by virtue of their sweep and range, they are capable of controlling both white and dark squares at the same time.*

White's weak Q-side Pawns have advanced to the point where they have difficulty protecting each other. While Black's K-Bishop ties White to the defense of his KRP, his comrade harasses the other wing.

Diagram 81

WHITE	BLACK	WHITE	BLACK
1 . . .	**B–K4**	5 K–K4	**P–R6**
2 P–N3	**B–B7**[1]	6 P–N4	**P–N6**
3 N–Q3[2]	**BxNch**[3]	7 PxP	**BxP**
4 KxB	**P–N5**	8 *White Resigns*[4]	

[1] Two Bishops work in better harmony than Bishop and Knight.
Note how Black's Bishop on K4 keeps a weather eye on both wings, whereas White's Bishop is lifeless and the Knight limited in scope.
[2] Threatening 4 N–B5ch.
[3] Black exchanges only because he sees the possibility of a forced win.
[4] White must lose a piece after P–R7.

The two Bishops or Time?

EVANS—LARSEN, U.S. OPEN CHAMPIONSHIP, 1949

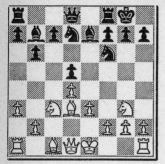

White moves. Granted that two Bishops are an advantage in the majority of positions—just how much is it worth going out of one's way to win them? Is it worth neglect of development and loss of Time?

Obviously, the answer depends on the given positions. As a general rule, Time is more important in open positions, whereas one can more easily afford to delay development in closed positions.

Diagram 82

WHITE	BLACK	WHITE	BLACK
1 N–B5[1]	R–K1	3 O–O	P–B4
2 NxBch	QxN	4 P–QN4	P–B5[2]

[1] Here the specific problem is whether White should castle or move an already developed piece (N–B5) in order to exchange it for a Bishop.

The order of White's moves is more than academic. If 1 O–O, R–K1; 2 N–B5, B–KB1—Black saves his Bishop! Black's Bishop serves a valuable function by guarding the dark squares. Since the position is sufficiently closed, White can afford to move his Knight a third time in order to "win" the Bishop. The course of the game, in fact, justified this strategy. For later developments see Diagram 23.

[2] If instead 4 . . . PxNP; 5 PxP, QxNP?; 6 N–N5! threatening N–B7 and/or B–R3, and B–K7 winning the Queen. Black has now established a protected, passed QBP—ordinarily a strong formation. However, White's two Bishops, plus the possibility of mobilizing his central majority by P–B3 and P–K4, give him a decided advantage.

Force or Time?

White moves. Many positions pose a real dilemma: repair Force and lose Time, or repair Time and lose Force? There is no blanket answer. The general rule is that Force is more important than Time and should be given preference in the absence of any other vital considerations.

Diagram 83

WHITE	BLACK	WHITE	BLACK
1 NxP[1]	B–N5ch	4 P–QR3	B–B4
2 K–B1	Q–Q4	5 P–R3	O–O[2]
3 N–B3	B–N2		

[1] Here the problem is whether White should castle or play NxP. In the first case he seems to lose a Pawn; in the second, he regains it but loses Time.

White fears that if he castles, Black can hold on to his QP by B–B4, hence he decides to repair Force even though it means he will have to move his King in the sequence. However, White, in this particular case, can have his cake and eat it too. He can go ahead and castle: e.g., 1 O–O, B–B4; 2 R–B1, B–N3; 3 B–K5, O–O; 4 NxQP, etc. (4 . . . BxN; 5 BxB, QxB?; 6 BxPch wins the Queen.)

Incidentally, it should be noted that Black cannot meet the text with 1 . . . QxN because of 2 BxPch, winning the Queen.

[2] Black has a splendid aggressive lineup against White's hapless King. Play continued: 6 B–K5, N–K5; 7 BxN, QxKB; 8 Q–K2, Q–B4; 9 N–Q4, BxN;10 BxPch, Bxfch; 11 KxB,Q–Q4ch;12 P–B3, QxB; 13 QxPch; K–R1; 14 Q–K2, R–B3 with an abiding attack.

Always snatch material—if you can do it and live!

BISGUIER—SHERWIN, ROSENWALD TOURNEY, NEW YORK, 1955

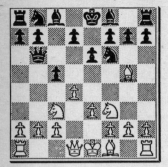

Diagram 84

Black moves. Scavenging for material while neglecting development is a typical beginner's fault.

White has just played N–QB3, offering his QNP. Black can ignore the "gift" by continuing his development with the placid B–K2—or he can face the challenge by plunging his Queen out-of-play. He takes the plunge and lives to tell the tale!

WHITE	BLACK	WHITE	BLACK
1 . . .	QxP[1]	5 N–B4	QxN![5]
2 N–N5	Q–N5ch	6 N–Q6ch	BxN
3 P–B3	Q–R4[2]	7 BxQ	PxB[6]
4 N–Q2[3]	P–QR3![4]		

[1] In chess lore there is a standing taboo against capture of the enemy QNP at the cost of development. As he made his move Sherwin said, "Why should I labor under antediluvian prejudices?" Bisguier merely smiled enigmatically. The test for snatching a dangerous Pawn is whether you see a way to get away with it, even if it means undergoing an arduous defense before your advantage in Force begins to manifest itself.

[2] Notice how Black returns his Queen quickly into play and uses it to prevent the threatened N–B7ch.

[3] Threatening N–B4 followed by N–Q6ch. Black seems to be in real trouble.

[4] A magnificent conception—as will be seen. There is an alternate defense: 4 . . . P–Q4; 5 N–N3, Q–N3; 6 B–KB4, N–R3; 7 PxP, BxP; 8 NxB, QxN; 9 B–Q6—Black is a Pawn ahead but White has adequate compensation inasmuch as Black will have enormous difficulty in castling.

[5] The point. Not 5 . . . Q–Q1; 6 N(5)–Q6ch, BxN; 7 NxBch, K–K2; 8 PxP regaining the Pawn and leaving Black's King hopelessly exposed in the center of the board.

[6] Time to take reckoning. Black has three pieces for the Queen—a tally of 105 units to 100 in the table of relative values. Once Black consolidated, he won easily.

The best way to refute a sacrifice is to accept it!

EVANS—SUSSMAN, NEW YORK METROPOLITAN LEAGUE, 1950

White moves. If a sacrifice is unsound, then naturally it must be accepted. If it is sound, there is little else to do about it.

Black has a formidable attack. White can capture either the Knight or the Bishop, neither of which looks any too appetizing in view of his exposed K-position. But he must capture—before Black's attack reaches overwhelming proportions.

Diagram 85

WHITE	BLACK	WHITE	BLACK
1 PxB[1]	NxPch	6 QxR	QxNch
2 K–N2	Q–N5ch	7 K–B1	Q–R6ch
3 N–N3	NxPch	8 Q–N2	Q–Q6ch
4 RxN[2]	BxR	9 K–N1	R–K1??[4]
5 Q–B3	R–K7ch?[3]	10 QxP mate	

[1] Not 1 PxN, BxP!; 2 KxB, Q–R7ch; 3 K–B3, RxN; 4 QxR, Q–N6 mate.

[2] This is no time to be greedy!

[3] Better is 5 . . . QxQch (if 5 . . . Q–N4; 6 R–KB1 holds everything); 6 KxQ, leading to an endgame with two pieces against Rook and two Pawns, which, however, is still in White's favor because of his powerful, passed QP. The text loses by force for Black.

[4] This monstrous blunder is explicable only by the fact that Black had to complete the requisite number of moves before the time-control. It is quite hopeless for him in any event.

The sword of Damocles

EVANS—HANAUER, U.S. CHAMPIONSHIP, 1951

White moves. Force can generally be used to win more Force! Here White has an extra Pawn. Black cannot afford exchanges. Yet the constant threat to exchange permits White to gain Time and make further inroads. We like to think of this process as the "sword of Damocles."

Diagram 86

WHITE	BLACK	WHITE	BLACK
1 R–K1[1]	R–B2	8 B–K3	N–B3
2 R–K5!	P–QR3[2]	9 R–KR4![4]	P–R3
3 R–B5ch	K–Q1	10 R–KN4!	N–R4ch[5]
4 B–N8![3]	P–QN3	11 K–R4	K–B3
5 R–B6	R–N2	12 R–N6ch	K–Q4
6 B–B4	K–Q2	13 RxQNP[6]	
7 R–B4	N–R2		

[1] Threatening to invade on K7. Watch how this Rook gradually makes inroads via the threat to exchange. White wants to exchange all the pieces, or Rook for Rook—not Bishop for Knight as then Black might have good drawing chances in the Rook and Pawn ending. Hence White abstains from the obvious 1 P–QR4, which would only drive the Knight to a good defensive post at QB2. White has no intention of exchanging Bishop for Knight just yet!

[2] Not 2 . . . N–B2; 3 R–QB5 which exchanges all the pieces and leaves White with an easily won King and Pawn ending.

[3] A study in technique! White threatens P–QR4 (the Bishop takes the retreat at R2 away from the Knight). This threat to exchange forces Black to weaken his Pawn Structure still further.

[4] Provoking further Pawn weaknesses.

[5] Or if 10 . . . K–K1; 11 R–N6.

[6] Winning a second Pawn, and the game came tumbling after.

Force can be converted into Space

EVANS—STEINER, 3rd MATCH GAME, 1952

Diagram 87

White moves. There is a saying that the hardest thing in chess is to win a won game. Here White is an exchange ahead but Black dominates Space. The key to the defense is the principle that an advantage in Force automatically carries an advantage in Time because each exchange benefits the stronger side. The threat to exchange means a gain of tempo.
Black menaces a draw. If it were his move, 1 . . . R–K7; 2 Q–B1, R–K6 would force a repetition.

WHITE	BLACK	WHITE	BLACK
1 R–R5!	Q–B6[1]	**3 R–N5**[3]	
2 R–B4!	Q–R6[2]		

[1] 1 . . . QxR; 2 QxR would completely ease White's defensive task. Black's only chance is to try and keep the game complicated. The point of White's defense is that Black's Queen has been forced to release the K-file, consequently R–K7 is no longer threatened.

[2] Again White has utilized the threat to exchange—this time to gain Space and to drive Black's Queen still further out of play. Notice how White is striving to coordinate his Rooks.

[3] White has brought his Rook into play and eased the immediate threat to draw. The rest, though difficult, is a matter of technique. White's passed QRP is the decisive factor. Without it the game would be drawn.

Here are the remaining moves: 3 . . . K–R2; 4 B–K4, K–R3; 5 BxB, PxB; 6 Q–B6, N–N2; 7 R–B7, Q–R7ch; 8 K–R3, Q–K3ch; 9 QxQ, NxQ; 10 R–B4, R–K7; 11 P–N4, R–K6ch; 12 K–N2, P–R5; 13 P–N5ch, K–R4; 14 R(5)–N4, P–R6ch; 15 K–R2, KxP; 16 R–R4, K–B4; 17 RxP, R–K7ch; 18 K–N1, P–N4; 19 R–R3, P–N5; 20 P–R5 (finally it starts to move), N–N4; 21 P–R6, N–B6ch; 22 K–B1, R–KR7; 23 P–R7, R–R8ch; 24 K–B2, Black Resigns.

Simplification

EVANS—LYMAN, HOLLYWOOD OPEN, 1954

Diagram 88

White moves. Simplification is a valuable defensive resource. When defending, each exchange eases the task of the defender because it means one less attacking piece to worry about.

White is an exchange ahead, but Black's terrible Knights threaten to ride roughshod over him. The immediate threat is 1 . . . NxQBP. White, moreover, is weak on the light squares and his Bishop has no scope. 1 RxN loses to Q–N8ch; 2 K–B2, QxRch. Clearly, forceful tactics are called for.

WHITE	BLACK	WHITE	BLACK
1 P–B5[1]	RxP[2]	3 Q–B8ch	K–B2
2 RxN![3]	RxR	4 R–B2ch	K–K2[4]

[1] This clearance sacrifice gives the Bishop scope. Because he is ahead in material, White can afford to sacrifice this Pawn to ease the pressure.

[2] After 1 . . . QxP; 2 QxQ, RxQ; 3 B–Q4 Black's attack has been stopped (because the Queens are off the board) and White's advantage in Force looms decisive (3 . . . NxB; 4 RxN, NxP; 5 R–QB2).

[3] The point. Black no longer has the retort Q–N8ch because he has been forced to block this diagonal by capturing the BP with the Rook.

[4] White has a ferocious attack even though he has returned the exchange and is a Pawn down to boot. 5 QxP should not now be played because of R–Q8ch. In the game White continued with 1 Q–B8ch. Actually, the winning move is 5 P–KR4! making "Luft" for the King and threatening B–N5ch. In any event White always has a draw in hand by perpetual check.

When ahead in Force, open lines

BERLINER—EVANS, U.S. OPEN CHAMPIONSHIP, 1950

Diagram 89

Black moves. If the general pattern for converting superior Force into victory is to exchange pieces, it follows that the opening of lines favors the player who is ahead.

Here, Force seems to be equal. However, this is only a mirage. Upon closer examination it appears that White's K-Bishop on KR1 is hemmed in and out-of-play. Hence, it remains merely for Black to rip open the Q-side lines. Note how quickly White's game disintegrates.

WHITE	BLACK	WHITE	BLACK
1 . . .	P–N3!	13 NPxP	K–B2
2 Q–B2	P–R4!	14 N–N1	K–K1
3 P–R3	PxNP	15 K–K1	K–Q1
4 RPxP	B–R3	16 K–Q2	K–B2
5 KR–B1	B–QN4	17 B–N4	K–N2
6 RxR	QxR	18 N–R3	B–Q1
7 R–R1	Q–N2	19 K–K1	K–R3
8 R–R3	R–QR1	20 N–N1	B–R4
9 Q–B3	B–B3	21 BxB	KxB
10 RxR	QxR	22 N–Q2	K–N5
11 Q–R3	QxQ	23 B–B3[1]	PxB
12 BxQ	NPxP	24 NxP	N–B3[2]

[1] Desperation. This Bishop is useless anyway.
[2] Black wins easily with his extra piece. Note how logically Black ripped open the Q-side and then penetrated via the open lines which he created.

The best defense is attack

SANTASIERE—EVANS, U.S. CHAMPIONSHIP, 1948

Diagram 90

Black moves. Black is a piece ahead but his pieces are undeveloped and his King has already been forced to move and thus has forfeited the privilege of castling. White threatens to rip open the KB file in order to get at Black's exposed King.
Should Black be tightfisted or liberal? The principle involved in defending is to return some Pawns in order to bring pieces into play. Extra material is no good unless it can be used!

WHITE	BLACK	WHITE	BLACK
1 ...	Q–R2![1]	7 QxP	Q–B7[4]
2 QxQP	R–Q1	8 N–Q2	QxBP
3 Q–N5	N–K2[2]	9 QR–B1	Q–R6
4 PxP	PxP	10 R–KN1	RxRch
5 BxP	R–N1ch	11 RxR	QxKP[5]
6 K–R1	R–Q4[3]		

[1] Black must be repulsed! There is no time for tightfisted moves like 1 . . . R–Q1; 2 Q–N6ch, K–B1; 3 B–R3!, R–Q3 (not 3 . . . QxB; 4 Q–B7 mate); 4 PxP. 1 . . . PxP would only help White by opening the KB file for him.
[2] Black must bring his pieces out. He should not even stop to worry about defending his QNP.
[3] This Rook—which does nothing in the original diagram—comes strongly into play.
[4] Always aggressive! Now Black actually threatens his own mate in one move. Compare this with the diagram and observe how Black has seized the initiative in return for three Pawns. Now he gets everything back with dividends.
[5] White's attack has been completely repulsed, Black is still a piece ahead, White's King is exposed. Black won shortly.

The Positional Sacrifice

The consequences of a positional sacrifice are supposed to unfold gradually, as in a Greek drama. The outcome is not always immediately apparent and often the only tangible return is pressure. Sometimes the motives of a positional sacrifice are so unclear that one is tempted to wonder whether it is intentional. At Carlsbad, 1907, Cohn was awarded the brilliancy prize against Tchigorin for a "beautiful combination starting from an extraordinary deep Pawn sacrifice." But Cohn admitted after the game that he had not intended to sacrifice the Pawn—he had lost it, after which he had been forced to play energetically to compensate for his material disadvantage!

An example of a "pure" positional sacrifice which, incidentally, has a strange genesis, occurs in the following variation of the Sicilian Defense:

WHITE	BLACK	WHITE	BLACK
1 P–K4	P–QB4	6 B–KN5	P–K3
2 N–KB3	P–Q3	7 P–B4	B–K2
3 P–Q4	PxP	8 Q–B3	P–R3
4 NxP	N–KB3	9 B–R4	P–KN4!?
5 N–QB3	P–QR3	10 PxP	. . .

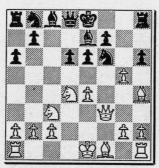

Diagram 91

Position after 10 PxP

This position saw the light of day at the International Tournament in Sweden, 1955, when three Argentinians met three Russians (by accident, in the same round) and sprung it as a prepared variation. The three Argentinians continued with **10 . . . KN–Q2** and lost with dispatch after **11 NxP!!, PxN; 12 Q–R5ch, K–B1; 13 B–N5!!** (13 . . . PxB loses to 14 O–Och, B–B3; 15 P–K5!, PxP; 16 N–K4.) Geller—Panno continued: 13 . . . N–K4; 14 B–N3!!, BxP; 15 O–Och, K–K2; 16 BxN, Q–N3ch; 17 K–R1, QPxB; 18 Q–B7ch, K–Q3; 19 QR–Q1ch, with a winning attack. It has since been found that **13 . . . R–KR2!!** holds.

After this triple massacre, the Argentinians (Najdorf, Pilnick, Panno) took the variation back to the workshop and came up with the new move: **10 . . . PxP; 11 BxNP, QN–Q2**—a positional sacrifice in the finest sense of the word because Black seems to have given up a Pawn and smashed his K-side without any compensation.

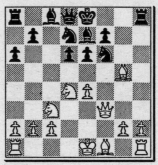

Diagram 92

Position after 11 . . . QN–Q2

Black does have considerable compensation for the Pawn. First, he has a highly compact Pawn mass in the center. Second, he has gained the square K4 for his pieces. Third, he controls all the open lines on the K-side (he will, of course, castle Q-side). Fourth, White has many weak squares. Whether this is sufficient for the Pawn, only tournament practice can decide.

The only criterion for a positional sacrifice is that it be *intentional*. The rest is a matter of judgment. Unlike the temporary sacrifice, whose aim is well-defined, the positional sacrifice has no clear-cut purpose. The result lies in the lap of the gods.

The Temporary Sacrifice

In contradistinction to the positional sacrifice, the temporary one has an immediate and tangible end. In his excellent book, *The Art of Sacrifice in Chess*, Rudolph Spielmann points out that there are two kinds of temporary tactical sacrifices: (1) the sacrifice for gain, (2) the mating sacrifice.

(1) The sacrifice for gain

WHITE	BLACK	WHITE	BLACK
1 P–K4	P–K4	5 O–O	B–K2
2 N–KB3	N–QB3	6 P–Q4	P–QN4
3 B–N5	P–QR3	7 B–N3	NxQP?[1]
4 B–R4	N–B3	8 BxPch!	

Diagram 93

Position after 8 BxPch!

	WHITE	BLACK
8	. . .	KxB
9	NxPch	K–B1[2]
10	QxN[3]	

[1] Correct is 7 . . . PxP.

[2] 9 . . . K–K3; 10 QxN, P–B4; 11 Q–B3, P–N5; 12 Q–N3 leaves Black's King far too exposed.

[3] White has regained his piece with interest. Black can no longer castle. White has an advantage in Space and Time.

(2) The mating sacrifice

WHITE	BLACK	WHITE	BLACK
1 P–K4	P–K4	5 P–Q4	B–N5
2 N–KB3	P–Q3	6 PxP	NxP?
3 B–B4	P–KR3?	7 NxN!	
4 N–B3	N–QB3		

Diagram 94

Position after 7 NxN!

If Black now plays 7 . . . BxQ, then 8 BxPch, K–K2; 9 N–Q5 mate. The mate can be averted, it is true, by 7 . . . B–K3, but in that event White merely remains ahead after 8 BxB, PxB; 9 Q–R5ch, P–N3; 10 NxP, N–B3; 11 Q–R3, etc.

Here, briefly, is another example—a trap in the French Defense which involves a mating sacrifice:

WHITE	BLACK	WHITE	BLACK
1 P–K4	P–K3	7 Q–N4	O–O
2 P–Q4	P–Q4	8 B–Q3	NxN
3 N–QB3	N–KB3	9 PxN	P–QB4
4 B–N5	B–K2	10 N–B3	P–B5?[1]
5 P–K5	N–K5	11 BxPch![2]	
6 BxB	QxB		

[1] This loses by force. Black has a satisfactory game after 10 . . . P–B4, P–B3, or P–KR3.
[2] A common maneuver. Black loses after 11 . . . KxB; 12 Q–R5ch, K–N1; 13 N–N5, R–Q1; 14 Q–R7ch, K–B1; 15 Q–R8 mate.

Piece against three Pawns

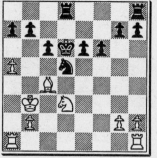

Diagram 95

White moves. In the middle game a piece is always superior to three Pawns. In the endgame, owing to its peculiar queening possibility, the Pawn increases in value.

This position is instructive—and difficult. If Black can mobilize his Pawns, he will have good winning chances. White has the advantage right now because the Pawns are relatively immobile.

WHITE	BLACK	WHITE	BLACK
1 KR–K1	P–K4[1]	11 RxR[5]	K–B2
2 QR–Q1	K–B2	12 R–KN8	N–Q6
3 N–B5	KR–K1	13 RxPch	K–Q3
4 R–K2	P–QN3[2]	14 K–B3	P–K5
5 PxPch	PxP	15 RxP	K–K4
6 N–R6ch	K–N2	16 R–R5ch	P–B4
7 R(2)–Q2	P–QN4?[3]	17 P–N4	P–N5ch
8 BxP	PxB	18 K–Q2	NxP
9 N–N4	NxN[4]	19 RxPch	K–Q2
10 RxR	RxR	20 P–N5[6]	

[1] Black should first build-up in the center with 1 . . . KR–K1. This push, though not fatal, weakens the white squares. In order to preserve his winning chances, White must keep some of his Pawns on the board. His immediate plan is to hold Black's center in restraint and try to compel weaknesses in what is now a sound Black Pawn Structure.

[2] Another weakness. But Black had to counter the threat of R(2)–Q2.

[3] The losing move. Black's game is difficult yet perhaps tenable if he gets out of the pin by 7 . . . R–QB1. He may be able to hold after 8 N–N4, NxN; 9 KxN, R–B2.

4 Black must either sacrifice the exchange (which he does) or end up with only two Pawns for the piece.

5 Ordinarily, Knight and 2 Pawns are a good match for a Rook, but here the Rook can penetrate to the K-side Pawns. Note how helpless the Knight is.

6 White now gets his passed Pawn moving. The remaining moves were: 20 . . . N–B5ch; 21 K–K2, N–K4; 22 R–B6, N–N5; 23 R–QN6, K–B4; 24 R–N8, NxP; 25 P–N6, N–N5; 26 P–N7, N–B3; 27 R–KB8, *Black Resigns*—the lone Pawn cannot be stopped.

Queen against uncoordinated minor pieces

KRAMER—EVANS, NEW YORK STATE CHAMPIONSHIP, 1949

White moves. Theoretically, White has material equality in two Rooks against a Queen—100 units to 100. But here his pieces are so scattered and Black's Knights so strongly placed that White is likely to lose a piece in trying to establish a line of communication. Black's immediate threat is 1 . . . NxB; 2 RxN, QxN. In order to meet this threat, White must lose a piece.

Diagram 96

WHITE	BLACK	WHITE	BLACK
1 N–B3[1]	Q–Q2	3 R–R4	P–B5![3]
2 R–K4[2]	P–B4	4 N–K2	Q–K2
		White Resigns[4]	

[1] If instead 1 B–N5, P–R3; 2 B–K7 (or B–R4), N–Q7!; 3 R–Q1, QxN; 4 RxN, Q–N8ch.
[2] To prevent QxPch.
[3] Preventing B–R6ch and renewing the threat of QxPch.
[4] White cannot meet the double threat of QxR and QxN.

Queen against coordinated minor pieces

Diagram 97

Black moves. *This is extremely difficult to evaluate at first glance. White has a Queen and three Pawns for a Rook and two pieces—130 to 120 units in White's favor.*

As a general rule the pieces win if they can coordinate and penetrate before the Pawns get far enough advanced to do any harm. Once the Pawns get mobilized the defender's pieces are nailed to the defense. So the pieces must be made aggressive at all cost.

In the actual game Black got panicky in time-pressure and walked straight into a lost ending after **1 . . . RxP?; 2 RxR, R–KB1; 3 QxRch, BxQ; 4 RxP.**

In reality Black has the better of it. Correct is **1 . . . R–KB1!** after which White must fight for his life. For instance:

If **2 Q–R3, N–K5!** **3 Q–K6ch, R–B2.**
If **2 Q–N4, R–B5** followed by **QR–KB1,** or **N–K5.**
If **2 Q–N6, R–B3** followed by **QR–KB1** with a strong initiative.

For another good example of coordinated pieces against a Queen, see Diagram 66.

Queen against two Rooks

Diagram 98

Draw. *This is the normal case. White is a Pawn ahead but he can make no progress because the Rooks are connected and maintain an invulnerable blockade on the second rank. Even when White succeeds in creating a passed Pawn on the Q-side it cannot get through the blockade. Thus, though White has a theoretical advantage of 110 to 100 units, he can make no headway. Draw agreed.*

Moral: connect your two Rooks!

CHAPTER FOUR: Space

When two opponents are well matched, it is not likely that one of them is going to lose material in the early stages of the game. Nor is it likely that either of them is going to ruin his Pawn Structure or fall too far behind in development. Generally, however, one of them will acquire an advantage (however slight) in Space—and it will probably be the one who conducts the White forces. The onus of securing a space advantage falls on the first player. When he cannot do this, Black is said to have equalized the game.

Space refers to the area *controlled*—not necessarily *occupied*—by the *striking* power of Pawns and pieces *beyond the fourth rank* (the frontier line). This is a general definition and does not apply to the endgame where the battle has generally shifted to the ends of the board.

Diagram 99

The frontier line

Diagram 100

The center

The Center

The idea of the opening is to bring all the minor pieces up to the frontier line so that they bear down particularly on your enemy's half of the center. The center is crucial and should be thought of as the core of the chessboard. When pieces or Pawns are placed in or near it they gain enormously in mobility. By controlling the center you cramp your opponent by forcing him to develop his pieces on inferior squares.

Mobility

Mobility is another expression for freedom of movement. When pieces occupy the center, they radiate greater mobility. For example, consider a White Knight on KB3 opposed to a Black Knight on QR3—the Knight on B3 strikes at 8 squares, whereas its counterpart strikes at only 4, or is 50 per cent less mobile. The same applies to the other pieces, proportionate to their distance from the center.

Diagram 101

Mobility

Diagram 102

Unoccupied Squares

Control of Unoccupied Squares

In diagram 102 White's Q5 is a key central square, despite the fact that it is unoccupied. Until his Pawn can be advanced to Q4, Black's K-Bishop will be confined to a dead diagonal. At the moment White observes Q5 three times (with Pawn, Knight, and Queen). In order to reinforce the advance of his Pawn to Q4, Black must first put an additional piece to bear on that square, either with B–K3 or P–B3, or both. The theme of the game from here on will be the conflict between Black's constant challenge in the center and White's attempt to maintain control there. *White temporarily controls Q5.*

A Typical Space Advantage

In the following variation of the Nimzo–Indian Defense White controls his Q5 in a different way—by occupying it: **1 P–Q4, N–KB3; 2 P–QB4, P–K3; 3 N–QB3, B–N5; 4 P–K3, P–QN3; 5 N–K2, B–N2; 6 P–QR3, B–K2; 7 P–Q5, O–O; 8 P–KN3, P–Q3; 9 B–N2, P–K4; 10 O–O, QN–Q2; 11 P–K4.**

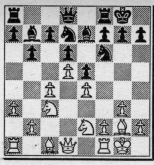

Diagram 103

Black is cramped. *White has a strong wedge of Pawns in the center. Black's position, being cramped, bears what Tarrasch termed "the germs of defeat." Black's best counterplay consists in N–K1 followed by P–N3 and P–KB4, but this still does not free his game or give his Bishops any life. The immediate 11 . . . B–R3 can be met with the simple P–N3. After 11 . . . P–B3; 12 PxP, BxP, Black has a glaring backward QP on an open file.*

Black might try to isolate White's QBP artificially by means of P–QR4, N–B4, P–R5, and B–R3, but this is too slow because White's comes first with the expansion P–QN4 followed by P–QB5 after appropriate preparation (N–QR4, B–K3, R–QB1, etc.). A positional player would play to strangle Black slowly to death, whereas an attacker might very well choose the double-edged tactical approach beginning with an early P–KB4.

How to Count Space

In Diagram 103 Black strikes at 4 squares past his fourth rank (Q5 and KB5 with his KP, K5 and KN5 with his Knight). White strikes at 7 and occupies 1 (White occupies Q5, strikes at QN5 with his Knight, KN5 and KR6 with his Bishop, QN5, QB6, K6, and KB5 with his Pawns). Thus, White has an advantage in Space by 8 squares to 4.

Stability

It is not enough merely to control or occupy Space—you must be able to retain it! Invasion or penetration *per se* means little unless the advanced troops can be maintained with a steady line of communication, a steady flow of supplies and reinforcement. Napoleon's *grande armée* isolated in the Russian campaign has its chess counterpart in a center which has been overextended. As we saw in a previous chapter, the question of overextension has been tossed into the theoretical cauldron by the Hypermoderns (e.g., Alekhine's Defense), but there are definite ways to test stability.

How to Test Stability

In the Sicilian Defense, after the moves **1 P–K4, P–QB4; 2 N–KB3, N–QB3; 3 P–KN3, N–B3; 4 P–K5?** would be a blunder because of N–KN5.

Diagram 104

White's artificially isolated KP cannot be maintained. White's KP is attacked twice and defended only once. White can lend it additional support by 5 Q–K2, whereupon Q–B2 wins the advanced Pawn. White can try to maintain this Pawn by tactical means: **5 P–Q4, PxP; 6 B–KB4,** *but now Black gets a beautiful game by* **N/5xKP!; 7 NxN, NxN; 8 BxN, Q–R4ch; 9 ANY, QxBch.**

The test of stability, therefore, depends upon whether the reinforcements of an advanced outpost (actual or potential) *exceed the means by which this outpost may be assailed.*

Thus armed, we are now equipped to tackle a more complex problem of modern theory—the Yugoslav Variation of the King's Indian Defense: **1 P–Q4, N–KB3; 2 P–QB4, P–KN3; 3 N–QB3, B–N2; 4 P–KN3, O–O; 5 B–N2, P–Q3; 6 N–B3, P–B4; 7 P–Q5.**

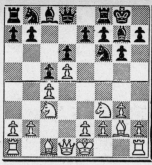

Diagram 105

Can White maintain his center? *To answer this question we must first ascertain what is meant by "center" and, having done that, investigate the ways by which Black can undermine this center.*

When we ask "can White maintain his center?" what we really want to know is whether White's Pawn on Q5 is a liability or an asset. Before we go into that, note that White has an advantage in Space (by count 8 to 6).

In the present position how is Black to undermine White's seemingly formidable center? 7 . . . P–K3 is the first possibility that leaps to mind, for after 8 PxP, BxP, Black attacks the QBP and threatens P–Q4. But if White ignores the move and continues with 8 O–O, PxP; 9 PxP, then Black has merely exchanged Pawns and come no nearer to an answer. No, what Black must do is *strike at the base* of White's Pawn chain—QB4—and potentially QR2 after White plays P–QN3. The way Black can accomplish this is by striving for an early P–QN4. Accordingly, Black might now essay the sophisticated maneuver **7 . . . N–R3** in order to reinforce P–QN4 by playing P–QR3 after the Knight has reached QB2 to give the advance additional support. The game might continue: **8 O–O, N–B2; 9 P–K4, P–QR3; 10 P–QR4,** and now Black is confronted with two alternatives—10 . . . R–N1; 11 P–R5, P–QN4; 12 PxPep., RxP with strong pressure on the QN file but with no hope of assailing White's central Pawn wedge; or—10 . . . P–N3 (to prevent P–R5); 11 R–K1, R–N1; 12 P–K5!, N–Q2; 13 B–B4 and White exerts tremendous pressure in the center before Black has time to get started with his flank attack.

Thus White *can* maintain his center because he can prevent P–QN4. Time is the crucial factor in his favor. If, in the diagram, Black's Knight were already on QB2 instead of QN1, then White's center would be untenable.

Centralize the King in the endgame

EVANS—KÖNIG, HASTINGS, 1949–50

Diagram 106

Black moves. *An advantage in Space and mobility is surprisingly enduring. Despite the reduction of forces, White wins because his pieces are better placed. Even without Knights he would win the King and Pawn ending. White's King is centralized, Black's is not; White's Knight is centralized, Black's is not. This powerful centralization is converted into the win of a strategic Pawn.*

WHITE	BLACK	WHITE	BLACK
1 . . .	N–B5[1]	6 P–N5	K–Q3
2 K–B5[2]	N–K6	7 P–N6	N–K4
3 K–B6[3]	K–Q1	8 P–N7	N–Q2
4 KxP	K–B2	9 N–K6	*Black Resigns[4]*
5 K–R6	N–B5		

[1] Black attempts to bring his Knight into play. The QNP is doomed anyway. If 1 . . . K–Q2; 2 K–B5.

[2] Avoiding a trap. If 2 NxP, N–K6ch; 3 K–K4 (forced), N–B7; 4 N–B3, NxP; 5 N–Q5ch, NxN; 6 KxN, K–Q2—Black draws—he has the opposition.

[3] A finesse. 3 KxP, K–Q3; 4 K–R6 is equally good. Black's reply is forced.

[4] If 9 . . . K–K4; 10 K–R7, KxP; 11 N–B5, NxN; 12 P–N8(Q).

Moral: the King is a fighting piece—use it!

Don't hem in Bishops

Diagram 107

Position after 3 ... N–KB3

White moves. A typical illustration of developing Bishops before pushing the King or Queen Pawns one square arises in the Q's gambit declined after the moves: **1 P–Q4, P–Q4; 2 P–QB4, P–K3; 3 N–QB3, N–KB3.** *White now has a choice between* **4 P–K3** *or* **B–N5.** *He should develop his Bishop first, so as not to lock it in.*

The principle of mobility is involved: Bishops are no good behind closed lines, and only in case of necessity should they voluntarily be hemmed in by their own Pawns.

Black's Q-Bishop is known as the "problem child" of this defense. The drawback of declining the Q's Gambit with 2 ... P–K3 is that this Bishop must eventually be freed either by placing it on QN2 or by striving for P–K4. Black's game is cramped but sound; yet this method of defending the Q's Gambit has lost popularity because it is too passive.

The Slav Defense is one way of declining without locking in the Bishop: e.g., **1 P–Q4, P–Q4; 2 P–QB4, P–QB3; 3 N–KB3, N–B3; 4 N–B3, PxP; 5 P–QR4** (to prevent 5 ... P–QN4), **B–B4; 6 P–K3, P–K3; 7 BxP, B–QN5; 8 O–O, O–O** and Black has freed both his Bishops.

Another way of freeing the Bishops is via the Q's Gambit Accepted: **1 P–Q4, P–Q4; 2 P–QB4, PxP; 3 N–KB3, N–KB3; 4 P–K3, P–QR3; 5 BxP, P–K3; 6 O–O, P–B4; 7 Q–K2, P–QN4; 8 B–N3, B–N2.**

Both these alternatives, however, have the drawback of permitting White to get in an early P–K4.

Restrain key freeing moves

Diagram 108

Position after 3 . . . B–N5

White moves. "Restraint" is a method of insuring a spatial advantage by preventing moves which would permit an opponent to expand. Conversely, it is a defensive tactic—to prevent an opponent from getting a spatial advantage in the first place. The Nimzo-Indian Defense (named after Aaron Nimzovitch) is a good example of what its founder termed "prophylaxis," or, as we know it, restraint. It arises after **1 P–Q4, N–KB3; 2 P–QB4, P–K3; 3 N–QB3, B–N5.**

Black's last move develops a piece, initiates an annoying pin, prepares castling, and, what is probably the most important facet of all, *prevents* White from expanding with P–K4. The point is that White must now hem in one of his Bishops. Probably best now is 4 P–K3. However, if White tries to bring out his Q-Bishop first, he gets into trouble: e.g., **4 B–N5, P–KR3; 5 B–R4, P–B4** followed by **Q–R4** with tremendous pressure on the QR4–K8 diagonal—especially since White's Q-Bishop can no longer play a role in defending these dark squares.

Every move in the world has been tried here for White, and still no way has been found to secure him more than a minimal advantage. Offhand, **4 P–B3** (menacing P–K4) looks good. This move, however, takes the best square away from the K-Knight, and can adequately be met by **4 . . . P–Q4** (5 Q–R4ch, N–B3).

When to decentralize

White moves. White has a minimal advantage in Space, and in order to preserve it he must prevent Black from playing . . . P–Q4. It is important for White to prevent this move—even if it means losing a tempo and withdrawing a beautifully centralized Knight.

In order to prevent the freeing action (. . . P–Q4) White must apply the principle of restraint. And the only satisfactory move is the paradoxical 1 N–N3! Let us see why.

Diagram 109

In order to understand the necessity of preventing Black from playing . . . P–Q4, let us examine what would happen if White ignored the threat and continued his development with **1 Q–Q2, P–Q4; 2 PxP** (2 NxN, PxN; 3 P–K5, N–K5! leads to full equality), **NxP; 3 NxKN, NxN!** (not 3 . . . QxN; 4 B–B3, Q-any; 5 NxN and Black's Pawn Structure is ruined); **4 BxN, QxN** and Black has completely freed his game.

Another unsatisfactory way of preventing . . . P–Q4 is with **1 B–B3.** For after **1 . . . N–K4** White would either have to retreat the Bishop to K2 (whereupon . . . P–Q4 would follow), or he would have to leave it there and suffer the loss of the two Bishops.

Incidentally, **1 NxN, PxN; 2 B–B3** would hardly help matters, for after **B–K3** White would still be unable to prevent P–Q4.

Therefore, the most feasible way for White to observe his Q5 is to put added pressure on it with his Queen, and the only way to do this is to withdraw an apparently well-centralized Knight: **1 N–N3!** Now the fight for . . . P–Q4 would continue after **1 . . . B–K3; 2 P–B4!** and Black will have to seek other moves (such as N–QR4) because **2 . . . P–Q4** is still unplayable because of **3 P–B5, B–B1** (even worse is 3 . . . PxP; 4 PxP, B–B1); **4 PxNP, RPxP; 5 PxP, N–N5; 6 B–B3** certifying the win of a Pawn.

Restraining the "minority attack"

D. BYRNE—EVANS, ROSENWALD TOURNEY, NEW YORK, 1954–55

Diagram 110

Black moves. White exerts pressure on Black's QP and he intends to undermine its base by playing P–QN4–5—the minority attack (see also Diagram 75). By the simple expedient of 1 . . . P–QR4 Black can either frustrate this strategy or make it very difficult to carry out. This move, it is true, would weaken QN3—but the square would be weakened anyway after the inevitable . . . P–QR3. The choice is really between a passive or an aggressive Pawn formation.

WHITE	BLACK	WHITE	BLACK
1 . . .	P–QR4[1]	4 R–N1[3]	B–KB4
2 O–O	R–K1	5 N–Q3	P–R3[4]
3 P–B3	B–B1[2]		

[1] We have seen that it occasionally pays to lose a tempo in order to restrain a maneuver that would cost far more Time to stop once it got started.

[2] This innocuous retreat prevents White from expanding with P–K4. In chess it is more important to frustrate your opponent's strategy than to be obsessed with your own sly designs.

[3] Faulty strategy. White wants to prepare P–QN4 and continue with the minority attack. Instead he should concentrate on enforcing P–K4. He hasn't the time to play for two ideas at once.

[4] Black has freedom for all his pieces—his last move was designed to make an escape square for the Bishop at KR2 after it is attacked. Note how White has failed to solve the problem of opening lines for his Q-Bishop.

Double-edged restraining moves

Diagram 111

Position after 6 P–QR4

Black moves. In the Q's Gambit Accepted after: **1 P–Q4, P–Q4; 2 P–QB4, PxP; 3 N–KB3, N–KB3; 4 P–K3, P–K3; 5 BxP, P–QR3** *experience has shown that White does better to castle and allow Black to play . . . P–QN4 than to try and restrain it with* **6 P–QR4.** *Why?*

White's last move is not bad, merely unnecessary. The principle behind it is good: restraint. But the move weakens White's QN4, and this can never be repaired. In other words, restraining moves are only good if they serve their function without fundamentally weakening the Pawn Structure. You must always keep the long-range prospect of the endgame in mind.

The game might possibly continue: **6 . . . P–QB4; 7 O–O, N–B3; 8 N–B3, B–K2.** It is true that Black will not be able to develop his Q-Bishop with ease. On the other hand, White has the same trouble developing his own Q-Bishop—and he has accepted a weak Pawn Structure to boot. Reshevsky-Fine, Semmering 1937, continued: 9 Q–K2, O–O; 10 R–Q1, Q–B2; 11 P–R3, R–Q1; 12 P–Q5, PxP; 13 BxQP, N–QN5 with satisfactory prospects for Black.

The "bind"

Black moves. A bind is a strangle-hold. It generally results after one player has acquired a weak square complex. This is a drastic example. Black's dark K-side squares are hopelessly weak. His King is hemmed in and he cannot meet the threat of R–R4 and QxPch. A bit pat, perhaps, but not if it gets across this point: constriction is bad.

Diagram 112

WHITE	BLACK
1 . . .	B–K5[1]
2 NxB	*Black Resigns*[2]

[1] Desperation. The idea is to meet 2 R–R4 by P–N4. The only other reasonable attempt at counterplay consisted of 1 . . . R–B7; 2 BxR, PxB; 3 R–R4, P–B8(Q); 4 QxPch, NxQ; 5 RxN mate.

[2] There is no satisfactory way to prevent N–B6 followed by R–R4 once more. Not to mention the fact that Black has given up a piece. Black made numerous errors. With proper play on the part of your opponent, you should never be able to tie him up so completely.

Fight a bind!

Diagram 113

Black moves. Violent counter-measures, even sacrifice, must be considered in order to shake off the far-reaching tentacles of a bind while there is still time. White threatens BxB, followed by N–N5–Q6—and gradually Black will be smothered by the on-coming Q-side Pawn mass. Black can free himself only by one move: 1 . . . P–K4.

WHITE	BLACK	WHITE	BLACK
1 . . .	P–K4[1]	9 Q–K4	QxQ
2 PxP	NxKP	10 BxQ	R–K1
3 NxP	NxN	11 N–B4	B–KB6
4 RxN	B–N5[2]	12 B–R7ch	K–B1
5 RxRch	RxR	13 RxRch	KxR
6 BxN[3]	BxB	14 B–B2	B–N7
7 R–K1	B–B3	15 P–QR4	Draw[4]
8 P–R3	B–R4		

[1] That this weakens—or even sacrifices—the QP is of relatively little moment. The important thing is to play it while he can still breathe and is in a position to profit tactically from the consequent opening of the lines.

[2] Life at last! The Bishop basks in its new-found freedom. Black has sacrificed a Pawn but he has considerable pressure against White's light squares (notably KB6).

[3] White does not like to give up the two Bishops. But the alternative, 6 BxP would be met by B–B6! E.g., 7 BxB, NxBch; 8 K–N2, BxB; 9 NxB, N–K8ch, winning the exchange.

[4] After 15 . . . B–R6; 16 N–Q3, B–K5; 17 P–N5, BxN; 18 BxB, BxP regains the Pawn and establishes opposite colored Bishops.

When cramped, exchange pieces

ROTHMAN—EVANS, PRACTICE GAME, NEW YORK, 1948

Diagram 114

Black moves. Exchanges provide elbow room. Sometimes it is necessary to adopt apparently outlandish measures in order to free a cramped position, but usually it is worth it.

Black has the better Pawn Structure—he has compensation for his doubled Pawns in the open QR file. White's backward QP is a glaring weakness, but how can Black get to it? If 1 . . . O–O; 2 P–R5 followed by R–N3 subject Black to a fierce attack.

WHITE	BLACK	WHITE	BLACK
1 . . .	B–N5ch![1]	4 B–Q3	B–B3
2 B–Q2	BxBch[2]	5 R–N3	P–N3[4]
3 QxB	N–K2[3]		

[1] What Black must do is free his K2 square in order to use it for maneuvering his pieces.

This solves the problem. Black takes advantage of the momentary pin on the QR file to exchange Bishops.
[2] Gladly!
[3] This Knight is headed for KB4 or Q4, as circumstances demand.
[4] Black has a bind on the white squares and White's QP is subject to heavy fire. Note how Black has relieved his cramp and obtained freedom of movement:

Freeing combinations

DONOVAN—EVANS, MARSHALL CHESS CLUB CHAMPIONSHIP, 1949–50

Black moves. Cramped positions contain extraordinary resiliency. Sometimes one move can bring the sleeping pieces all to life.

This position arose out of the K's Indian Defense, yet note the similarity to Alekhine's Defense (Diagram 7). The freeing principle consists in striking at an overextended center from the flank. Black converts Time (the move) into Space.

Diagram 115

WHITE	BLACK	WHITE	BLACK
1 . . .	P–QB4![1]	5 BxN	BxB
2 O–O[2]	PxQP	6 NxB	Q–Q5ch
3 BxP	PxP	7 K–R1	QxN
4 PxP	NxP!	8 Q–B3[3]	

[1] This move rips White's center to shreds.

[2] White chooses a speculative Pawn sacrifice rather than see his center utterly destroyed after 2 PxQP, PxP; 3 BxQP, BxB; 4 NxB, NxP, though this was, objectively, his best line.

[3] White has some pressure for the Pawn inasmuch as Black will have trouble developing his Q-Bishop. Here Black should play 8 . . . R–QN1 followed by . . . P–QN3 and gradually his extra Pawn will come of age.

A wing attack is best met by a reaction in the center

KAGETSU—EVANS, HOLLYWOOD OPEN, 1954

Black moves. The attacker does not always benefit from open lines. He should try to close the center before embarking on a wing attack. This cannot always be done. The defender must keep his lines of communication open, and this requires a fluid center so that he may divert pieces from the other wing to the defense of the attacked wing.

Diagram 116

WHITE	BLACK	WHITE	BLACK
1 . . .	P–Q4![1]	4 P–KR4	BxN
2 QxN[2]	B–Q3	5 BxB	Q–N5
3 O–O–O[3]	R–N2[4]	6 B–Q2	PxP[5]

[1] Temporarily Black is a Rook ahead—but he is skating on thin ice, as will be seen.

If it were White's move, Black would be lost! E.g., 1 QxN followed by Q–B3, Q–R5, and Q–R7ch, against which there is no adequate defense. In order to frustrate this maneuver Black must somehow be able to get his Queen to the KR file by playing . . . QxP. However, this Pawn is presently protected by the Knight. In order to capture it the Knight on KB4 must first be dislodged. In order to do this Black must get his Bishop to Q3. Via this long chain of reasoning, Black arrives at the general principle that a wing attack is best met by a reaction in the center. The text frees the Q3 square for the Bishop.

[2] Best. 2 PxP is met easily by B–Q3. 2 NxP is met by QxP.

[3] White has no time for 3 Q–B3, BxN; 4 BxB, PxP; 5 BxP, B–N2!

[4] The pressure is off and finally Black has time to breathe. The object of this "mysterious" Rook move is not so mysterious. Black anticipates 4 Q–B3 Which would now be met by BxN; 5 BxB, QxP (otherwise the Rook on N1 would be attacked).

[5] It's all over but the handshake. Black now whipped up a winning attack very quickly: 7 R–N1, Q–K3; 8 B–K2, Q–R7!

Connect Rooks

Diagram 117

Black moves. This principle is very simple. It merely states that the ideal of development is to clear all the pieces off the first rank until the Rooks are connected. In this way both Rooks are free to occupy open files, especially in the center. When the Rooks are connected in this fashion, it generally heralds the end of the opening and the beginning of the middle game.

WHITE	BLACK	WHITE	BLACK
1 . . .	B–Q2[1]	5 B–Q2	P–KR4[5]
2 Q–N3[2]	QR–K1[3]	6 R–K1[6]	RxRch
3 Q–Q1[4]	R–K2	7 BxR	N–Q5
4 N–B3	KR–K1	8 N–K4	Q–B4[7]

[1] Black has reached his maximum development. He should take advantage of the lull to develop his Q-Bishop, even if only to so modest a square as Q2. What this does is release the Q-Rook, thus accomplishing the connection.

[2] This only loses several tempi. White is already far behind in development, and he should prepare to free his Q-Bishop by playing 2 N–B3 immediately.

[3] This is an ideal move. It develops a piece which is out-of-play with gain of time. Nothing more could be asked.

[4] White's Queen is misplaced anyway. If instead 3 N–B3, P–N3, then the threat of N–Q5 forces the Queen to move again. White has a Time advantage. The problem now is to exploit it before it evaporates.

[5] This Pawn is to be used as a battering ram, to provoke some weaknesses in White's K-side Pawn Structure.

[6] It is always a good policy to challenge on the file before the opponent's control of it becomes too dominating.

[7] White's game is still extremely difficult. Black's pieces are beautifully posted.

The wrong Rook

EVANS—COLLINS, LOG CABIN CHESS CLUB CHAMPIONSHIP, 1950

Diagram 118

White moves. When Rooks are connected and either of them can occupy a necessary central file, annotators are in the sarcastic habit of writing "the wrong Rook!" no matter which one moves there.

Here either of White's Rooks can move to Q1. Once his QP is bolstered from behind, then White will be able to constrict Black's game with P–K4. The question is: which Rook should be played to Q1, and why?

WHITE	BLACK	WHITE	BLACK
1 KR–Q1[1]	QR–B1	4 P–K5[3]	N–Q4
2 QR–B1[2]	Q–N1	5 N–K4	R–B2
3 P–K4	P–QN3	6 N(K4)–Q6[4]	

[1] This move follows certain sound, though never before formulated, rules. When either of two Rooks can move to a necessary central file, these are the criteria to be applied: (1) select the Rook which is doing the least; (2) select that Rook which, after it arrives there, will permit the remaining Rook its greatest possible mobility. *Before selecting your move, it is important to visualize on which central files each Rook will do the most good.*

Here White chooses the K-Rook because he foresees that he wants a Rook on QB1 and a Rook on Q1. Moreover, if he moved his QR to Q1 he would violate rule number 2—after it gets there the K-Rook would only have one square to which to move (K1), whereas now the QR has two squares (QN1 and/or QB1).

[2] Completing the development of the Rooks and exerting masked pressure on Black's Queen. Black can do little but sit back and wait. His position is cramped but quite solid.

[3] Again, White gives to get. He cannot maintain the tension in the center forever. A good alternative is 4 Q–K2, with the idea of playing for a break with P–Q5.

[4] Black's Knight on Q4 is his only well-posted piece. White, on the other hand, has completed an invasion deep into enemy territory and has a bind on the dark colored squares. Note how Black's pieces get in each other's way.

"Sitting on" a position

White moves. *It is not always necessary to do something when you have an advantage. Nowhere is patience more a virtue than in chess. One of the most common fallacies is the assumption that every move must contain some vicious threat. In the absence of direct tactical combinations, one should take advantage of the lull to develop pieces or, if they are already developed, to find even better squares for them.*

Diagram 119

WHITE	BLACK	WHITE	BLACK
1 QR–Q1[1]	P–B4[2]	3 BxB	RxB
2 QxQ	NxQ	4 P–B3[3]	

[1] This move "sits on" the position. It exerts masked pressure on the Q-file, brings a Rook into play, and discourages the freeing maneuver, P–Q4. Incidentally, the reason White's QR moved to Q1 rather than his KR is explained in the previous illustration. The first question White must ask himself is "where do I want my Rooks?" He wants his QR on Q1 and his KR on K1. If he played 1 KR–Q1, where would he put his QR later on?

[2] 1 . . . P–Q4 is refuted by 2 BxN, BxB; 3 PxP, QxP (forced); 4 N–B3 and Black's doubled QBP's are robbed of the little mobility that they now possess.

[3] White has lasting pressure in the center, control of Q5, and good play against Black's disconnected, doubled, Q-side Pawns. But Black should be able to hold this end game.

"Luft"

Black moves. "*Luft*" *(German for* "*air*") *is breathing space—i.e., an escape square—for the king. It can come in very handy.*

This position is drawish, but the skirmish is far from over. White has a qualitative majority on the Q-side (3 Pawns to 2). Before proceeding any further, both sides take advantage of the lull to make "Luft."

Diagram 120

WHITE	BLACK	WHITE	BLACK
1 . . .	**P–KR3**	**2 P–KR3**[1]	. . .

[1] Neither side now has to worry about an impromptu mate on the last rank. They are now free to embark on their business for the day. Why not 1 . . . P--KN3; 2 P–KN3? The reason is that these moves would weaken too many squares. For greater detail consult Diagram 55.

The King and Pawn ending resulting from this position after all the pieces have been exchanged is analyzed in Diagram 156. Just for the fun of perfecting your endgame technique, remove all the pieces and play this position out with a friend. It is a theoretical draw.

"My kingdom for a Luft!"

White moves. Failure to make Luft can have disastrous consequences. White played 1 RxRP? and learned the hard way. Correct is 1 P–KR3 or—even better—1 P–KB3! gaining Time by the attack on Black's Knight.

Diagram 121

WHITE	BLACK	WHITE	BLACK
1 RxP?[1]	RxR	5 K–B1	B–R3ch
2 RxR	R–B8	6 K–N1	P–R3![4]
3 N–B2[2]	N–B4	7 RxB	NxR[5]
4 P–B3[3]	B–Q3		

[1] White should content himself with a draw by 1 P–B3, RxR; 2 RxR, N–B4; 3 B–B2, etc.

[2] 3 K–B1 is refuted by B–N5.

[3] Too late! If White's Pawn were already on KR3, White could save everything by getting out of the pin with K–R2. As it is, he just has to suffer in silence. He is hoping for 4 . . . NxB?; 5 RxB—but no such luck.

[4] Black pays his tribute to the "Great God Luft." White now has no way to meet the threat of 7 . . . NxB; 8 RxB, RxN other than by sacrificing the exchange.

[5] White resigned shortly.

Escape squares

White moves. An "escape square" is an alternate expression for Luft when making a haven for a piece other than the King.

Sooner or later White will have to guard against . . . N–KR4. In order to insure that his Q-Bishop stays posted on the excellent diagonal which it now occupies (KR2–QN8), White should play **P–KR3** *in order to retreat the Bishop to R2 when challenged.*

Diagram 122

1 P–KR3 was played in the game on the supposition that it was necessary sooner or later. Actually, it is not immediately necessary because N–R4 can be met with 2 B–K5, P–B3; 3 B–N3, NxB; 4 RPxN, with good attacking chances along the KR file.

However, White has nothing better to do. He might try the developing move, 1 R–QB1. He most certainly does not want to play 1 B–Q3 because PxP; 2 BxBP would force him to lose a tempo with the Bishop. One other good point of White's move is that it restrains Black's Q-Bishop by taking the square KN5 away from it.

Incidentally, since every Pawn move creates a new weakness, such a move should not be made without good reason (especially when it involves a loss of Time before development has been completed). This is a relatively closed position, so the loss of Time involved in 1 P–KR3 is negligible.

This diagram arises from a standard line in the Gruenfeld defense: 1 P–Q4, N–KB3; 2 P–QB4, P–KN3; 3 N–QB3, P–Q4; 4 B–B4, B–N2; 5 P–K3, O–O.

Overprotection

Black moves. Black's highly mobile center exerts a cramping influence on White's awkwardly placed pieces. It is important to maintain this center without advancing either KP or QP until all the pieces are prepared to demolish the potential blockade. Thus 1 . . . P–K5 immediately would be met by N–Q4, saddling Black with a backward QP.

Diagram 123

Black should overprotect his QP now with **1 . . . B–K3,** on the principle that White will gang up on it sooner or later. This move not only develops a piece, but also leaves White in doubt as to which Pawn will advance. The QP is then "overprotected" because, strictly speaking, Black has more pieces defending it than are actually necessary for its safety.

The game continued: 2 N–N5, B–B1; 3 P–KN4 (3 N–B3 is better), P–Q5; 4 PxP, NxQP; 5 K–N1, P–R3; 6 N–R3, N–B6; 7 RxR, KxR; 8 R–N3, N–Q7ch; 9 K–B1, NxB: 10 NxN, NxP, winning a Pawn. Note how Black converted his great influence in the center into material advantage.

Overprotecting weak points

EVANS (U.S.A.)—NIELSEN (DENMARK), DUBROVNIK OLYMPICS, YUGOSLAVIA, 1950

Diagram 124

White moves. Nimzovitch confined his concept of overprotection to key points in the center. We may extend it to any weak point anywhere on the board. White has white square weaknesses on KB3 and KR3. He can repair them with the temporizing **1 K–N2.** *In such a complicated position, this move looks quite innocuous. But it actually came in handy later and made possible the winning combination!*

WHITE	BLACK	WHITE	BLACK
1 K–N2	N–B4	8 NxN	R–QB3[3]
2 Q–N1	P–K3	9 RxN!	RxQ[4]
3 B–N5	R–K1	10 R–Q8ch	B–B1
4 B–Q2[1]	N(4)–Q2	11 BxR	K–N2
5 PxP	RxP	12 N–Q7	Q–Q4
6 N–Q5![2]	RxR	13 B–N5	B–N5[5]
7 QxR	QxP	14 R–N8ch	*Black Resigns*

[1] This finesse is a common maneuver. The Bishop, of course, was headed for Q2 all the time. By moving to N5 first it gained a tempo by forcing Black's Rook to an inferior file.

[2] Initiating a "masked attack." (See also Diagram 149.)

[3] Forced. If instead 9 . . . NxN; 10 R–Q8ch wins.

[4] Finally 1 K–N2 is vindicated! This little "combino" would not be possible with the King on N1 because Black would capture the Queen with check. Of course, White did not foresee this when he made his first move. It is a stroke of luck— serendipity.

[5] Note how helpless Black's Queen is against the minor pieces.

The Pawn as battering ram

EVANS AND SPIELBERGER—LOKVENCZ AND PRAVDA, CONSULTATION
GAME, VIENNA, 1956

Diagram 125

White moves. Black's Q-side looks pretty solid. White must force a point of invasion (see also Diagram 60). To do this he must use his Q-side Pawns as battering rams. It is amazing how quickly Black's position falls apart as soon as White obtains undisputed spatial control of the QN file, and, with it, the vital QN6 square—which gives him a base from which to strike at Black's backward QP.

WHITE	BLACK	WHITE	BLACK
1 P–QR4[1]	P–QR4[2]	8 QxQ	RxQ
2 PxBP	NPxP	9 R–N6![4]	K–K2
3 R–N2	R–N1	10 R–R6	R–N2
4 RxR	QxR	11 N–N5	N–K1
5 R–N1	Q–B2	12 NxP!	R–N6[5]
6 Q–N2![3]	R–B1	13 BxP	RxB
7 Q–N6	K–B1	14 N–N7 dis. ch	
			Black Resigns

[1] The threat of 2 P–R5 forces Black further to weaken an already compromised Q-side Pawn Structure.

[2] To prevent P–R5 Black cedes White control of QN5. Equally hopeless was 1 . . . PxP; 2 RxP, R–N1; 3 QR–N1, winning the QNP.

[3] Black must not be allowed to challenge the file with R–QN1. White's advantage in Space (undisputed control of the QN file) is now decisive.

[4] Control of this "jumping-off" point is crucial. The Rook cannot be stopped from its foraging mission.

[5] Or if 12 . . . NxN; 13 BxP wins. Note how powerfully White's two Bishops came into play when lines were opened for them.

Securing advanced outposts

EVANS (N.Y.)—QUESADA (HAVANA), RADIO MATCH, 1947

White moves. White wants to win the square KB4 for his Knight—an excellent post indeed. The fact that Black is not yet castled permits him to do it with **1 P–KR4.** *Ordinarily, this could be met by* 1 . . . P–KR3, *maintaining the Pawn on KN4. But here the pin is fatal, because after* 2 PxP *Black cannot recapture. All this trouble because Black has failed to connect his Rooks!*

Diagram 126

WHITE	BLACK	WHITE	BLACK
1 P–KR4!	**PxP**[1]	**3 N–B4**[2]	
2 RxP	**O–O–O**		

[1] Slightly better is 2 . . . P–N5 which, it is true, weakens the dark squares. But the text makes even a graver concession by allowing White a base of operations on the open KR file.

[2] The Knight has secured this outpost and cannot be dislodged. If necessary, it can be reinforced by bringing the QN to K2. Black has isolated K-side Pawns; White has a bind on the KR file. He won shortly.

Occupying advanced outposts

Diagram 127

White moves. Black is a Pawn behind but he has two Bishops and strong pressure. (White's Queen cannot defend both the Knight and the QP indefinitely.) The immediate threat is 1 . . . R–K1. White's Knight is passive and overburdened. But there is a ray of light.

White has a potential outpost on K5! How can he redeploy his Knight so that it can reach this radiant paradise!

WHITE	BLACK	WHITE	BLACK
1 N–N1![1]	R–K1[2]	3 RxR	QxR
2 N–B3	R–K2	4 N–K5[3]	

[1] The horse beats a strategic retreat. It is headed for K5 via B3.

[2] One move too late! If the Knight were still on K2, then White's maneuver would be impossible: e.g., 2 N–N1, RxR; 3 RxR, QxP.

[3] White's extra Pawn is now decisive—with his Knight on K5 he can go to sleep—his game plays itself. The remaining moves were: 4 . . . Q–QB2; 5 R–QB1, P–QR3; 6 P–KR4, Q–R2; 7 R–Q1, Q–N2; 8 K–R2, Q–R2; 9 Q–QB2, BxP; 10 QxP, R–QN1; 11 N–B6, Black Resigns.

CHAPTER FIVE: Time

Time (or tempo) is the unit of the move—it is the element of tactics. *The move is so vital that if a player with only mediocre ability were granted the right to move twice in a row, at his option, just once every game, he could become World Champion!*

"Time" is hard to define. Roughly speaking, it amounts to mobility and development. The ideal opening is one in which pieces are cleared rapidly from the first rank so that the Rooks are free to shuttle toward the center. One symptom of lost Time is a cramped position: when the moment arrives to make necessary developing moves (in order, for instance, to prepare for castling) the pieces can no longer develop on active squares. Time is equivalent to the "serve" in tennis; unless pursued vigorously, it is likely to dissipate. This "driving force" is termed the initiative.

The "initiative" is a Time advantage, and the first move confers this automatically on White. After **1 P–K4,** for example, White already threatens to control the center with **2 P–Q4.** Black, like it or not, is compelled to adapt his strategy to the threat. **1 . . . P–K4** meets it and also opens up lines for the Queen and Bishop. White, it is true, can still play **2 P–Q4, PxP; 3 QxP,** but he has moved his Queen too early and must now lose a tempo after **N–QB3.** There is no constructive square for the Queen: if to **Q1,** then nothing has been gained; if to **Q2, Q3, K3,** or **QB4,** then it would block a Bishop diagonal. **4 Q–R4** is relatively best, but then the Queen is out-of-play on the flank. In either case White is forced to delay the necessary development of one of his minor pieces for a move. In the meantime Black can develop another minor piece. Thus he has wrested the initiative.

Diagram 128

Black gains a tempo. *From this it may be concluded that whenever the same piece is forced to move a second time in the opening a* *tempo is lost. For this reason early Queen moves are inadvisable; the opponent can drive it from pillar to post in the course of normal development. If, after 1 P–K4, P–K4; 2 P–Q4, PxP, White does not wish to submit to the above loss of Time, he may elect to continue with the gambit 3 P–QB3?!*

Gambits

A gambit is an early attempt to seize the initiative forcibly (usually at the cost of a Pawn or two). The gambiteer hopes to profit from his rapid development and superior mobility to score an early victory, or to regain his material with interest. But it stands to reason that if the second player has made no organic weaknesses or errors such optimism is totally unfounded. There are three ways to meet a gambit: (1) declining it, (2) holding doggedly on to the sacrificed material at the cost of the initiative, (3) accepting it and then returning the material at a favorable moment.

Diagram 129

The gambit declined

1st *method*—Declining the gambit: **1 P–K4, P–K4; 2 P–Q4, PxP; 3 P–QB3, P–Q4.** (3 . . . P–Q6 also declines but does not force White to lose time in recapturing the Pawn, as 4 BxP develops a piece in the process).

With **3 . . . P–Q4** Black has opened more lines for his Queen and Q-Bishop. *He has elected to fight White in his own element—Time against Time!* A likely continuation is: **4 KPxP, QxP; 5 PxP, N–QB3; 6 N–KB3, B–N5** (notice how Black systematically exploits White's isolated QP by undermining the pieces which defend it); **7 B–K2, O–O–O** (not 7 . . . BxN; 8 BxB, QxQP?; 9 BxNch, PxB; 10 QxQ); **8 N–B3, Q–QR4** with lasting pressure against White's central Pawn as well as superior development.

124

2nd method—Holding doggedly on to all material sacrificed:
1 P–K4, P–K4; 2 P–Q4, PxP; 3 P–QB3, PxP; 4 B–QB4 (the
"Danish Gambit"; where White sticks to the true spirit of it, he
does not stop for 4 NxP but aims instead for quick development at
all costs), **PxP; 5 BxP, P–QB3.**

Diagram 130

The gambit accepted

With **5 . . . P–QB3** Black announces his intention of submitting
to an attack because he has the firm determination that White does
not have sufficient compensation for the two Pawns sacrificed.
Black is fighting White in another element—Force against Time!
Here the question is whether Black can withstand the fury of White's
attack and emerge into the won endgame which his material
superiority promises. Notice how Black has not yet developed one
piece, whereas White has two Bishops bearing down on menacing
diagonals. Black, however, has no organic weaknesses in his Pawn
structure and probably—though this is problematical—has sufficient
resources to defend with. The game might continue: **6 N–QB3,
P–Q3; 7 N–B3, N–Q2: 8 O–O** or **8 Q–B2** followed by O–O–O. If
White cannot capitalize on his advantage in Time, Black will nullify
it by catching up to him in development. The final evaluation of
this position is a question of style: an attacker would choose White;
a defender, Black. Tournament practise has indicated that White
has won the majority of the games continuing from the diagram
position—although in every instance one can point to a flaw in
Black's play.

3rd method—returning material at a favorable moment: **1 P–K4, P–K4; 2 P–Q4, PxP; 3 P–QB3, PxP; 4 B–QB4, PxP; 5 BxP, P–Q4.**

Diagram 131

The gambit accepted—and returned

The principle behind **5 . . . P–Q4** is so powerful that it has virtually eliminated all gambits from tournament play! *Black fights White in yet another element—Pawn Structure against Time!* Black returns the material in order to simplify and reach a favorable endgame.

A likely continuation is: **6 BxP** (6 PxP closes the lines and leaves Black a Pawn ahead with an easy defense after 6 . . . N–KB3; 7 N–KB3, B–Q3; 8 O–O, O–O; 9 N–B3, B–KN5; 10 Q–Q4, QN–Q2. Opocensky—Réti, Baden, 1914), **N–KB3!; 7 BxPch, KxB; 8 QxQ, B–N5ch** (the temporary sacrifice of a Queen is a good example of a strategical theme bolstered by tactical execution); **9 Q–Q2, BxQch; 10 NxB, P–QB4** and Black has a slight advantage theoretically because his Q-side Pawns are likely to move faster than White's K-side Pawns (it is easier to force 2 passed Pawns with 3 against 1 than 4 against 2—moreover, Black's King is a strong defensive weapon where it stands). Because of the opposite colored Bishops the game is likely to eventuate in a draw, but if this is the best White can obtain, obviously he will abandon the Danish Gambit.

The principle of accepting and then returning the gambit at a favorable moment has this most important corollary—it upsets the whole psychology of the attacker, it throws him on the defensive when he is in precisely the opposite frame of mind! For this reason it is a recommended antidote.

126

Refrain from useless checks

EVANS—FLORES, MARSHALL CHESS CLUB CHAMPIONSHIP, 1946–47

Diagram 132

White moves. A check is loss of Time if it forces the defender to make a necessary consolidation and leaves the checking piece in no better position than before. Ordinarily, a check does gain a tempo, provided that no unit can interpose which forces the retreat of the checking piece. (Diagram 136 is a good example of a check which gains Time.)

WHITE	BLACK	WHITE	BLACK
1 Q–R4ch[1]	B–Q2![2]	5 BxN	PxB
2 Q–N3[3]	N–B3[4]	6 QxNP[6]	R–QN1?[7]
3 P–K3[5]	N–QR4	7 QxRP	RxNP
4 Q–N4	NxP	8 N–B3[8]	

[1] An ingenious double-edged check whose consequences are difficult to foresee. Every move should have a purpose, and check is no exception. "Always check—it may be mate" is one of those glittering epigrams which belongs in the garbage heap. Checking merely for the sake of giving a check is a good way of working out spite, but is often likely to rebound.

[2] Black has many ways to go wrong and only one good interposition. If 1 . . . P–B3; 2 BxN, RxB; 3 QxP, B–B4; 4 P–B5, winning a Pawn. If 1 . . . N–B3; 2 N–N5 is difficult to meet. The text is played on the principle of interposing a unit which forces the retreat of the enemy piece. It leads to interesting complications.

[3] White had, of course, anticipated the Bishop interposition. He has lost a tempo but seems to gain it back if and when Black moves his Bishop again to QB3 in order to defend the double threat of QxP or PxP.

[4] Continuing the counterattack.

[5] White cannot forever neglect his development. 2 QxP, PxP! gives Black strong counterplay. And 2 PxP is met by QNxP.

[6] 6 QxBP is too tame and would merely lose the two Bishops without any corresponding compensation. White tries to get compensation in Force and Pawn Structure—hence the risky text.

[7] Here Black finally goes wrong. Correct is 7 . . . Q–N1!; 8 QxQ, RxQ. Black, it is true, is left with doubled Pawns, but he also has two Bishops and pressure on the QN file. 7 . . . Q–N1 is so strong that the whole variation has been abandoned for White.

If White knew at the time that 1 Q–R4ch was contrary to general principles, one is tempted to ask why he did it. The answer lies in the ever-constant search for innovations. Each position is as distinct as a fingerprint, and the modern master spends his leisure time in searching for refinements which capitalize on this distinctness. Even when a new move is inferior, it has the merit of catching an opponent off guard, as in the present game, where Black does not find the right continuation.

[8] White is a Pawn ahead. Black still has the initiative left over from his previous advantage in Time, but the course of the game showed that this compensation was insufficient. E.g., 8 . . . B–B3; 9 BxP, Q–B1; 10 B–N3, O–O; 11 O–O (White must bring his King to relative safety, even though his Pawn Structure is about to be shattered on the K-side), BxN; 12 PxB, Q–B3; 13 P–K4—White is quite safe.

Wasted moves

Diagram 133

Black moves. We generally think of a move as "wasted" when there is no particular plan behind it. At times it involves a precious loss of tempo in a position which cannot afford it. At others, while not an outright error, perhaps, it is totally unconnected with the requirements of the position; this is more often the case with beginners. As a case in point, witness my very first tournament game.

Black played **1 . . . P–KR3**—a wasted move if ever there was one. Let us see why.

To begin with, it contributes nothing toward development. Black has still to castle, and then he faces the problem of freeing his Q-Bishop. Furthermore, this move has no bearing on the action taking place in the center.

A good move is 1 . . . PxP. Black can make it hard, if not impossible, for White to regain the Pawn: e.g., 2 N–Q2, N–N3.

1 . . . O–O (though not so sharp as PxP) at least contributes toward the connecting of the Rooks which, as we have learned before, is the ideal of development.

The only justification for 1 . . . P–KR3 is that it prevents a pin at KN5. But why go to the trouble of preventing it? Once White's Bishop goes to KN5, then P–KR3 would effectively break the pin by "putting the question to the Bishop."

Refrain from pointless threats

Diagram 134

Black moves. A common failing of the beginner is that he makes unsound threats and then bites his nails hoping his opponent will overlook the right continuation. This is shabby chess; even if it succeeds, it only speaks poorly for the loser. If you really want to improve, always assume that your opponent will find the best reply and plan your play accordingly: "play the board not the player."

Never offer traps that are likely to rebound. White threatens mate in one. Watch how, with proper defense, this explodes in his face and results only in loss of Time.

The above position arises out of: **1 P–K4, P–K4; 2 B–B4, B–B4; 3 Q–R5.** White's last move with the Queen is a premature sortie— even though it contains the double threat of either QxP mate or QxKPch. However, this threat can be met quite easily by **3 . . . Q–K2.** Now if **4 N–KB3, P–Q3; 5 O–O, N–KB3**—and Black now gains a free developing move by harrying White's misplaced Queen.

In other words, *minor pieces should be developed before major pieces: Knights before Bishops.*

Complete development first—attack later

STEINER—EVANS, 6TH MATCH GAME, 1952

Diagram 135

Black moves. An attack is likely to boomerang unless adequate measures have been taken to prevent a successful counter-attack.

Black has an advantage—namely, the two Bishops. Eager to force an early decision, White leaves his King in the center and initiates a premature K-side attack with 1 P–KN4. Note how cleverly this is refuted.

WHITE	BLACK	WHITE	BLACK
1 . . .	N–B4[1]	3 NxN	Q–R5
2 N–K5[2]	NxBch	4 P–KR3	P–KB4[3]

[1] This move completely nullifies White's attack and wins the initiative.

[2] Forced. 2 PxN, BxNP wins a Pawn, and White has no way to bring additional support to his pinned Knight.

[3] Black has exchanged a passive Knight for an active Bishop. He has seized the offensive on the K-wing.

Developing with gain of Time

MECHANIC—EVANS, MARSHALL CHESS CLUB JUNIOR CHAMPIONSHIP, 1946

Diagram 136

Black moves. It is obvious that Black must move his K-Bishop so that he can castle. The question is where? 1 . . . B–K2 is sound, but not forceful enough. The trick is to find some way to take advantage of White's hanging Knight on K4. 1 . . . B–N5ch gains a tempo because it forces White to retreat, whereupon Black can castle. Two moves for the price of one!

WHITE	BLACK	WHITE	BLACK
1 . . .	B–N5ch![1]	3 P–QR3?[2]	B–K2[3]
2 N(4)–Q2	O–O		

[1] 1 . . . Q–R4ch would be met by B–Q2—and instead of losing a tempo, Black would gain one!

[2] "Putting the question" neither gains nor loses Time. It merely drives Black's Bishop to a better square. Better was 3 B–Q3 immediately.

[3] Black is actually ahead in development. White must free his Bishop and castle. Black has only to free his Q-Bishop—he has already castled. It is unusual for Black to seize the initiative so early. That he can do so indicates that White has made an error in the opening.

Exchanging with gain of Time

Diagram 137

Black moves. This position arises after: **1 P–K4, P–K4; 2 N–KB3, N–QB3; 3 B–B4, N–B3; 4 P–Q4!?, PxP; 5 O–O?!, NxP; 6 N–B3!?** *Black is now confronted with a dilemma. He can take the piece with PxN, or he can pursue orderly develop-ment with* 1 ... *NxN followed by B–K2. He should choose this method, since he is already sufficiently ahead in Force and must now make haste to repair his disadvantage in Time.*

WHITE	BLACK	WHITE	BLACK
1 ...	NxN[1]	**3 PxP**	P–Q4
2 PxN	B–K2[2]	**4 B–Q3**	O–O[3]

[1] This exchange gains a tempo by attacking the Queen. Other moves, though perhaps playable, lead to arduous defense:

   I. 1 ... PxN; 2 BxPch!, KxB; 3 Q–Q5ch, K–K1; 4 R–K1!, B–K2; 5 RxN, P–Q3; 6 B–KN5, with a fierce attack.

   II. 1 ... N–Q3; 2 N–Q5!, NxB; 3 B–N5, B–K2 (3 ... P–B3; 4 BxP!, PxB; 5 N–N5!, threatening Q–R5 mate) and Black has reasonable survival chances after 4 NxB, NxN; 5 BxN, KxB (not 5 ... QxB; 6 R–K1).

   III. 1 ... N–B3: 2 N–KN5, P–Q4; 3 NxQP, NxN; 4 Q–B3.

   IV. 1 ... P–Q4; 2 BxP, NxN; 3 BxNch, PxB; 4 PxN, PxP; 5 N–Q4, with a strong initiative.

[2] This is still no time to stop for booty with 2 ... PxP; 3 Q–Q5! Black should be content to return the Pawn—for he will still be a Pawn ahead—which is decisive once he completes his development.
[3] Black has brought his King to safety and is a Pawn ahead. That the analysis in note 1 is not completely convincing is beside the point. Since 1 ... PxN is not playable, Black should choose that defense which is natural and permits him to develop normally.

   Moral: *when confronted with several alternatives, seek the simplest one, if it takes you out of your troubles.*

Aggressive defense

Black moves. Black is two Pawns ahead but not at all happy. White has two threats; either 1 B–Q4 or 1 QxKBP (if 1 . . . PxQ; 2 RxP mate!).

It is Black's move—this is the only thing which saves him. This is no time for passivity. He must find an aggressive defense!

Diagram 138

WHITE	BLACK	WHITE	BLACK
1 . . .	Q–K7![1]	5 RxR	QxRch
2 QxKBP?[2]	QxB[3]	6 KxQ	Q–B5ch[4]
3 QxPch	K–R1	7 K–any	RxQ
4 R–B6	RxPch!		

[1] The only defense! This counterattack assures Black of a draw by perpetual check. But now White gets too ambitious.

[2] Correct was 2 B–Q4, forcing Q–B6ch; 3 K–R3, Q–N5ch; 4 K–N2, Q–B6ch, etc., with a draw.

[3] Of course not 2 . . . PxQ; 3 RxP mate.

[4] *Der Punkt!* Black now regains his Queen, simplifies, and remains a piece ahead.

Counterattack

●

EVANS—HARTLEB, U.S. OPEN, 1948

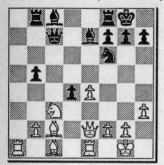

Diagram 139

White moves. When confronted with several alternatives, select the aggressive one (if it is sound). Passive positions limit mobility and should be avoided.

Black seems to have a promising position. He attacks the Knight, which can either retreat to Q1 (too passive) or advance to Q5, in which case 1 . . . NxN; 2 PxN, B–Q3 leads to an equal position. 1 NxP is refuted by RxN; 2 QxR, QxB. What, then, is the way out of White's dilemma?

WHITE	BLACK	WHITE	BLACK
1 P–K5![1]	PxN[2]	4 B–B4	Q–B4[4]
2 PxN	BxBP	5 P–QN4![5]	Q–N3
3 Q–K4![3]	P–N3	6 BxR[6]	

[1] White ignores his attacked Knight and applies the principle of counterattack. He thus touches off a forceful combination based on the momentary alignment of Black's Queen and Rook on the same diagonal.

[2] If the Knight gives way by 1 . . . N–K1; then 2 N–Q5, Q–Q2; 3 Q–K4, P–N3; 4 QxP wins a Pawn for White.

[3] The point! Black must lose material owing to the double threat of QxP mate and/or B–B4.

[4] Not 4 . . . Q–N3; 5 BxR, PxP; 6 R–R8, B–B4; 7 Q–QN4! BxB (if 7 . . . RxB; 8 R–K8ch mates); 8QxRch!; KxQ; 9 B–Q6dbl. ch. K–N2; 10 B–B8ch, K–N1; 11 B–R6ch, B–Q1, 12 R–K8 mate.

[5] A sharp finesse. If immediately 5 BxR, PxP!; 6 R–any, B–B4 and Black regains all his material with interest.

[6] The game continued: 6 . . . B–B4; 7 Q–KB4, QxB; 8 QxQ (when ahead in material, simplify!), RxQ; 9 BxB, PxB; 10 R–R6, B–N4; 11 R–QB6, B–Q7; 12 R–K5, P–B5; 13 K–B1, R–R1; 14 RxP, R–K1; 15 K–N1, R–K8ch; 16 K–R2, R–KB8; 17 P–B3, B–K6; 18 P–R4, B–B7; 19 R–N5ch, K–B1; 20 R–KR5, K–N2; 21 K–R3, P–B3; 22 K–N4, K–N3; 23 R–N5ch, K–B2; 24 R–N5, B–Q5; 25 R–N7ch, K–N3; 26 P–R5ch, K–R3; 27 R(6)–B7, P–B4ch; 28 KxP(B5), Black Resigns.

Sustaining the initiative

EVANS—FLORIDO, U.S. OPEN CHAMPIONSHIP, 1953

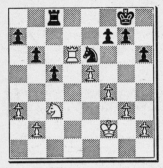

White moves. White has momentary control of the Q-file, which Black threatens to challenge by playing R–Q1. White must find some way to secure his spatial advantage or else lose the initiative. It is his move.

What White must do is to create weaknesses in Black's Q-side Pawn Structure, continually making new threats, so that Black has no time for R–Q1. Note that 1 R–Q7 is insufficient because of R–B2.

Diagram 140

WHITE	BLACK	WHITE	BLACK
1 N–N5![1]	P–QR3[2]	4 N–Q5	P–QN4
2 N–B3[3]	R–Q1[4]	5 N–B7	N–K3
3 RxRch[5]	NxR	6 NxRP[6]	

[1] This does the trick. Now Black has no time for R–Q1. He must advance his RP, and thus weaken his QNP in the process.

[2] Forced. 1 . . . R–R1; 2 R–Q7, P–R3; 3 N–Q6 leads to a decisive spatial advantage.

[3] The deed is done. Now Black must lose a Pawn because of his shaky formation. Note how the base of his Pawn Structure (on QR2) has been undermined.

[4] 2 . . . R–N1 is met by 3 N–Q5, winning a Pawn.

[5] Black gets too much counterplay after 3 RxP, R–Q7ch; 4 K–K3 (4 K–N1, N–Q5! threatening N–B6ch), RxRP. The moral is that when there are two ways to accomplish a given end (in this case, the win of a Pawn), that method which allows your opponent the least counterplay should be selected.

[6] White wins a Pawn. The rest is technique. The game continued: 6 . . . P–B5; 7 K–K3, K–B1; 8 P–B5, N–Q1; 9 K–K4 (notice the importance of a centralized King), N–B3; 10 P–KN4, K–K2; 11 K–Q5, N–R4; 12 N–B7, P–B6; 13 PxP, N–B5; 14 NxP, N–K6ch; 15 K–Q4, NxNP; 16 P–R3, N–B7; 17 P–QR4, NxP; 18 P–R5, K–Q2; 19 P–R6, K–B3; 20 P–R7, K–N2; 21 P–K6, PxP; 22 PxP, Black Resigns.

Interpolations

BRONSTEIN (U.S.S.R.)—EVANS (U.S.A.), TEAM MATCH, MOSCOW, 1955

Diagram 141

Black moves. An interpolation is an in-between-move. Before making a forced move (in this case Black's Rook is attacked and must retreat sooner or later), a finesse may be inserted. (See Diagrams 12 and 13 for the classic example.)

If he retreats the Rook immediately, there is no way for Black to prevent P–K4. By first interpolating **1 . . . B–B4** *Black also gains a tempo.*

WHITE	BLACK	WHITE	BLACK
1 . . .	**B–B4**	5 RxN[2]	**BxR**
2 P–K4!?[1]	**B–N3ch**	6 QxB	**QxB**
3 K–R1	**RxP!**	7 B–N1	**R–Q1**[3]
4 NxR	**NxN**		

[1] Now or never—even at the cost of a Pawn. After 2 Q–B1, R–K2 Black retains a permanent bind in the center. Bronstein correctly reckons that White's best chance lies in active counterplay (at the cost of a Pawn) rather than passive defense.

[2] Forced. Black was threatening N–N6ch.

[3] Black is a Pawn ahead. White did not now go in for 8 Q–R7ch, K–B1; 9 Q–R8ch, K–K2; 10 QxNP, QxBP; 11 R–K1ch (not 11 RxQ?, R–Q8ch; 12 R–B1, RxR mate), with a possible draw. The game ended in a draw anyway due to the presence of opposite colored Bishops.

"Zwischenzug"

Diagram 142

Black moves. "Zwischenzug" is a German endearment reserved for the more aesthetic cases of interpolation, such as this.

Black can play 1 . . . QxP; 2 PxB, QxP; 3 QR–B1 and White will have good open lines as compensation for his Pawn minus. Whether he likes it or not, it seems that Black will have to enter this variation. After all, his Queen is attacked and it must move —must it not?

WHITE	BLACK	WHITE	BLACK
1 . . .	N–Q5!![1]	**3 PxB**	N–B7
2 Q–K3[2]	QxP	**4 Q–N3**	NxR[3]

[1] A "Zwischenzug" in its full glory! Black ignores the attack on his own Queen and blithely proceeds to counterattack.

[2] The amazing thing is that White's Queen has no haven. If—

I. 2 Q–Q3, Q–N5!; 3 PxP (if 3 PxB, N–K7ch followed by NxB), N–K7ch; 4 K–R1, NxB; 5 PxR(Q), NxQ!; 6 QxP (forced), B–Q5 followed by NxPch and wins.

II. 2 Q–B1, Q–N5; 3 PxP (if 3 PxB, N–K7ch; 4 K–R1, NxB wins a piece), N–B6ch!; 4 K–R1, QxB (threatening mate); 5 P–KN3 (if 5 PxN, B–K4; 6 Q–N2, QR–N1 winning a piece), Q–R3! and Black inevitably emerges from the complications a piece ahead.

III. 2 Q–K4, QxP; 3 QxQ, PxQ; 4 PxB, N–K7ch; 5 K–B1, NxB.

IV. 2 RxN, QxR; 3 PxP (if 3 PxB, QxB,) QR–K1; 4 P–N8(Q), RxQ(K7) and Black wins owing to the double threat of QxPch and/or RxQ.

[3] Now that Black has won material the rest is easy. The game continued: 5 RxN, KR–K1; 6 P–KR4, Q–K5; 7 R–Q1, QR–Q1; 8 RxR, RxR; 9 B–K5, R–K1; 10 B–Q4, Q–N8ch; 11 K–R2, QxP; 12 P–KB4, P–QR4; 13 P–B5, Q–Q4; 14 PxP, RPxP; 15 Q–B4, Q–KB4; 16 Q–R6, P–B3; 17 Q–Q2, R–K5; 18 Q–R2ch, K–N2; 19 Q–B4, Q–B5ch; 20 P–N3, Q–B6; 21 Q–B7ch, K–R3; White Resigns.

Converting Time into Pawn Structure

MAYER—EVANS, U.S. JUNIOR CHAMPIONSHIP, 1949

Black moves. Black is a piece down. He can recapture immediately, but there is no rush. The fact that it is Black's move gives him a Time advantage. He must seek a way to convert the less durable element (Time) into the more durable one (Pawn Structure). The judicious use of an interpolation accomplishes this end.

Diagram 143

WHITE	BLACK	WHITE	BLACK
1 . . .	BxNch[1]	6 K–Q2	N–N3
2 PxB	KxB	7 KR–K1	KR–K1
3 P–B3	P–B4	8 B–B2	N–B5ch
4 B–K3	K–B3	9 K–Q3	N–R6
5 R–QN1	N–Q2[2]	10 RxR	RxR[3]

[1] 1 . . . KxB is too tame. It would give White time to defend himself with 2 B–Q2, and if QR–K1ch; 3 N–K2. (Even so, Black can probably still win with . . . BxBch; 4 KxB, N–K5ch; 5 K–K1, R–K3; 6 P–B3, QR–K1; 7 PxN, RxP, regaining the piece with interest.) Black now has a winning endgame.

[2] The Knight is headed for QB5—occupying the hole. 5 . . . KR–K1 first is also quite good.

[3] White is lost. His white squares are hopelessly weak and his doubled Pawns are useless. The game continued: 11 R–N2 (relatively better is 11 R–K1), P–B4; 12 B–N3?? (this loses by force, though there is no escape from the bind), N–B5; White Resigns. There is no defense either to NxR or R–K6 mate.

139

Converting Time into Space

STEINER—EVANS, HOLLYWOOD OPEN, 1954

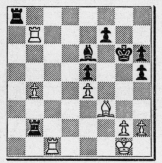

Diagram 144

Black moves. Timing is always essential. If it were White's move, 1 P–KR3 would render his position impregnable. Likewise, after 1 . . . R(1)–R7; 2 P–KR3 stops Black cold. It is imperative that Black first undermine White's defender—the Bishop— before invading on the seventh rank. This is all made ripe by **1 . . . B–N5!**

WHITE	BLACK	WHITE	BLACK
1 . . .	**B–N5!**	**5 K–B1**	**R(N7)–N7**
2 R–B1[1]	**R(1)–R7**	**6 K–N1**	**R–N8ch**
3 P–R4[2]	**BxB**	**7 R–B1**	**RxRch**
4 RxB	**RxPch**	**8 KxR**	**R–R7**[3]

[1] 2 BxB, PxB leaves White equally defenseless against R(1)–R7. There is no defense against this threatened spatial incursion.

[2] Forced. 3 BxB allows mate in three.

[3] Winning a second Pawn. This is a good example of the conversion of Time into Space into Force.

The pin is mightier than the sword!

McCORMICK—EVANS, MARSHALL CHESS CLUB CHAMPIONSHIP, 1946–47

Diagram 145

Black moves. The pin is a combination Space–Time advantage. Time in the sense that the pinned piece is momentarily tied down; Space in the sense that the piece which is pinned is not free to advance.

Here Black's Bishop is pinning White's QBP. How can this be exploited?

WHITE	BLACK	WHITE	BLACK
1 . . .	**P–QN4!**	**3 NxNch**	**NxN**
2 N–Q5[1]	**PxP**	**4 Q–R3**	**PxP**[2]

[1] Nothing helps. White cannot avoid the loss of at least a Pawn. 2 NxP, P–QR3 gains Black a piece based upon yet another infernal pin.
[2] Black has won a Pawn and all his pieces have sprung to life. White, however, achieved considerable counterplay. For the culmination of this game, see Diagram 138.

Pins do not run away

Black moves. Very often the beauty of a pin is that there is no hurry about converting it into a Force advantage because the pinned piece cannot run away.

White is a Pawn down but he has pressure. With one blow Black can shatter his game by initiating a brilliant pin.

Diagram 146

WHITE	BLACK	WHITE	BLACK
1 . . .	NxP!	4 BxR	R–K1[3]
2 RxN	P–Q3![1]	5 B–B3	R–K5![4]
3 B–B3	RxRch[2]		

[1] 2 . . . BxR; 3 QxB would merely result in Rook and two Pawns for two pieces. But Black is hunting for bigger game. There is no rush to capture the Rook until White moves his Queen in order to break the pin. White, however, is not given so much as one free move in the sequence.

[2] Again, there is no rush. The pin will not run away.

[3] Still no rush to play . . . BxR. White must now defend his Bishop.

[4] The point. White must now lose a full Rook because of the pin. 6 QxR, PxQ; 7 RxP, Q–B4 yields White insufficient material for the lost Queen. And if 6 RxP, QxR; 7 QxB, QxB wins.

Moral: exploit pins to the utmost—be in no rush to release them. Restraint is one of the most difficult habits for the average player to acquire. It's not enough to find the right move—but the right moment as well.

Hidden pins

Black moves. Not all pins are obvious. In fact, in this position it is hard to tell which of White's pieces is pinned—even potentially!
Black's Bishop is attacked. An unimaginative player might withdraw it and be content.

Diagram 147

WHITE	BLACK	WHITE	BLACK
1 . . .	N–R6ch[1]	3 PxQ	BxP
2 K–B1	QxQ	4 R–Q2	B–R5[2]

[1] A player who has read this page will by now be alerted to the fact that White's KNP is pinned. Pinned now, no. But pinned after the text. The Pawn cannot capture the upstart because it is wedded to the Queen.

[2] White is a Pawn behind and his Pawn Structure is shattered.

I expect that any player who has gotten this far in the book will be able to win in the ensuing endgame.

"Putting the question" to the Bishop

This happy phrase owes its existence to Nimzovitch, who perceived that pins—even potential ones—should be broken immediately. They are always dangerous.

Whenever convenient recaptures are possible, and "putting the question" does not seriously impair the Pawn Structure, take time out to do it!

Diagram 148

Position after 3 . . . P–QR3

Black's last move seems like a waste of Time. What is its purpose?

Well, **3 . . . P–QR3** says, in effect, either exchange or retreat—but declare your intentions! By "putting the question" Black stops the Bishop from serving three functions at the same time: (1) pinning, (2) controlling the KB1–QR6 diagonal, (3) controlling the QR4–K8 diagonal. The consequences of **4 BxN, QPxB; 5 P–Q4, PxP; 6 QxQ, QxQ; 7 NxQ** do not favor White (see Diagram 16). Whereas, **4 BxN, QPxB; 5 NxP, Q–Q5** permits Black to recapture his Pawn under favorable circumstances.

The major merit of **3 . . . P–QR3** is that it eases the pressure against Black's KP. After **4 B–R4**, Black should not go chasing after the Bishop with **4 . . . P–QN4** because it unnecessarily weakens the Pawn Structure. He should continue his development with **4 . . . N–B3**. The fact that White's Bishop is on R4 instead of N5 means that the pin can be broken now in only one move (P–QN4) instead of two (P–QR3 and P–QN4). This can come in handy. For instance, after **5 O–O, B–K2; 6 P–Q4?, PxP; 7 NxP?, NxN; 8 QxN, P–QB4; 9 Q–any, P–QN4; 10 B–N3, P–B5** winning the Bishop (Noah's Ark Trap). Of course this trap is not the justification of **3 . . . P–QR3**; it is just a handy interpolation which has nothing to lose and everything to gain.

Masked attacks

EVANS—JIMENEZ, CUBA INTERNATIONAL TOURNEY, 1952

White moves. A masked attack is an indirect pin. There are two meaningful ones here: (1) White's Rook exerts a masked attack against Black's Queen, despite the fact that four men intervene; (2) White's Bishop exerts a masked attack against Black's Rook, despite the intervention of a Pawn and Knight. White must seek a way to open both lines at the same time.

Diagram 149

WHITE	BLACK	WHITE	BLACK
1 P–K5!	PxP[1]	4 NxB	RxN[2]
2 N–B6	Q–B1	5 N–K7ch	*Black Resigns*
3 PxP!	B–Q1		

[1] This offer can neither be accepted nor refused! If instead 1 . . . B–N2; 2 N–B6, Q–B1 (forced); 3 N(6)–K7ch, RxN; 4 NxRch wins the Queen by a fork.

[2] Equally hopeless is 4 . . . QxN; 5 N–B6ch.

CHAPTER SIX: Quiz!

Caution

This quiz is not an artificial concoction. All thirty-six illustrations are flesh and blood, so to speak, taken, as they are, from practical tournament play. This is a new type of quiz; it is not intended to be easy, nor to gratify the solver's ego. You will be asked for the broad strategical principles underlying each position. Knowledge of these principles is more important than that of specific moves. The answers will refer you back to the diagrams where they are discussed. Even if you have mastered all the previous material, do not expect to score 100 per cent, nor even 80 per cent, because the solutions are not invariable and rigid. There are too many parts to each question, and, therefore, they are impossible to grade.

Thus far we have spoken of abstractions: Pawn Structure, Space, Force, and Time. Now that we have analyzed chess in terms of its jigsaw components, the problem is to put them all back together again and to play a creditable game. The biggest difficulty in the quiz will doubtless be recognizing what principle is applicable to any given position. Your approach should be logical. Ask yourself under what heading the question falls, select what you think is the best move, and try to justify it in terms of the above abstract principles.

Chess is an art form, and there is a lot of room for variation and dissent. However much you may disagree with my reasoning on a given principle, I beg you to remember that it works. That is its only justification. When any principle ceases to bring results, the time has come to abandon it. The only thing revolutionary or "new" about my system is that it has never before been formulated in this manner.

Diagram 150

Is P–KR3 appropriate for White. Why? Why not? What are the principles involved?

Diagram 151

What is Black's best move? On what principle?

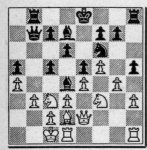

Diagram 152

What is Black's best move? On what principle?

Diagram 153

Where are White's holes? What is Black's best move? On what principle?

Diagram 154

What is Black's best move? On what principle?

Diagram 155

What is Black's best move? On what principle?

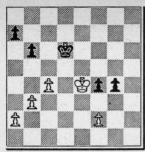

Diagram 156

Who has the "outside passed Pawn?" Black to move—what is the result?

Diagram 158

Where is the base to Black's QP? Who has the "better" Pawn Structure?

Diagram 160

White is weak on what color squares? What are 3 sharp ways for Black to exploit this weakness?

Diagram 157

What shot disrupts Black's Pawn Structure?

Diagram 159

Which is better: 1 . . . P–Q3 or 1 . . . P–Q4?

Diagram 161

Who has the "good Bishop" and why?

Diagram 162

Where does Black have a "hole?" How can White exploit it to win a Pawn?

Diagram 163

Black wins a Pawn. How? On what principle?

Diagram 164

How can White convert his Space advantage into Force?

Diagram 165

White wins a piece. How? On what principle?

Diagram 166

How can Black capitalize on White's weak squares to win a piece?

Diagram 167

Why is 1 QxP an error?

Diagram 168

How can Black exploit White's weak KN1–QR7 diagonal to win material?

Diagram 169

On squares of which color is White weak? What is Black's winning motif?

Diagram 170

What is White's most forceful continuation? On what principle?

Diagram 171

How can Black win a Pawn by a pin?

Diagram 172

Why is 1 P–K4 premature?

Diagram 173

White moves—who has the bind?

Diagram 174

How should Black recapture? On what principle?

Diagram 175

How can Black exploit White's QBP? On what principle?

Diagram 176

Who has the better game? Why?

Diagram 177

How can White quickly mobilize his Q-Rook in the center?

Diagram 178

How can White mobilize his center Pawns?

Diagram 179

Is 1 P–K4 playable? Why? Why not?

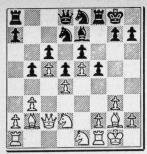

Diagram 180

Black has just played P–KB4. Should White capture *en passant*? Why? Why not?

Diagram 181

Black has just played P–N3. Why is this inferior?

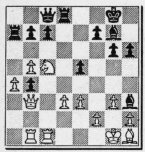

Diagram 182

White moves. He has a winning interpolation. What is it?

Diagram 183

Which is more accurate: 1 O–O or 1 Q–B2?

Diagram 184

What is Black's best move? On what principle?

Diagram 185

Which is more accurate for Black: 1 . . . P–QR4 or 1 . . . P–K5?

Solutions to Quiz

(Diagram numbers refer to location of principle involved)

(150) EVANS—HEINKENHEIMO, HELSINKI OLYMPICS, 1952. (See Diagrams 108, 119, 120.)

Yes. White has reached his maximum of normal development. **1 P–KR3** makes Luft, prepares an eventful B–K3 by forestalling the reply N–KN5, thus restricting the enemy Knight. The main principles involved are "Luft" and "restriction." The alternative, 1 N–KR4, B–Q2 accomplishes nothing since it leaves the Knight out on a limb.

(151) EVANS—SANDRIN, U.S. OPEN CHAMPIONSHIP, 1949. (See Diagram 42.)

1 . . . PxP—on the principle of leaving White with a backward BP exposed to an open QB-file. White must now recapture with his KP.

Score yourself wrong if you thought that 1 . . . O–O was correct, on the principle of completing development. Then after 2 O–O, PxP (too late!); 3 BPxP! and White has had time to straighten out his Pawn Structure.

Also inferior, while we're on the subject, is 1 . . . P–B5; 2 B–N1, followed by an eventual steamroller in the center with P–B3 and P–K4.

(152) BERLINER—EVANS, U.S. JUNIOR CHAMPIONSHIP, 1946. (See Diagram 66.)

1 . . . P–B5—on the principle of attacking a Pawn chain at its base. The move is tactically justified in view of 2 QPxP, BxN; 3 BxB, NxKP. (*Not*, however, 1 . . . PxP?; 2 PxP, RxR; 3 RxR, NxNP?; 4. NxB, BPxN; 5 QxN, PxN; 6 R–R8ch, K–K2; 7 Q–N5ch, P–B3; 8 QxP mate.)

(153) PLATER—EVANS, HELSINKI OLYMPICS, 1952. (See Diagram 57.)

White has a hole on his Q3—not to mention QR3, KB3 and KR3! Black should hamper White's development with **1 . . . Q–Q6**, occupying the hole and preventing the freeing move, P–Q4. White now struggled like a harpooned whale and succeeded in repulsing the blockade only by incurring further weaknesses on his light squares: e.g., **2 P–KB4, N–B3; 3 PxP, B–N5; 4 B–B3, BxB** (White's Bishop was needed for defense); **5 RxB, NxP; 6 R–B1, P–KN4!?** (one of those double-edged restraining moves which weakens the Pawn Structure to prevent N–B4). **6 . . . QR–Q1** is also quite good.

(154) PILNICK—EVANS, MARSHALL CHESS CLUB CHAMPIONSHIP, 1949–50. (See Diagram 40.)

1 . . . P–QB4—on the principle of repairing an isolated Pawn. White's backward QBP is now doomed: e.g., **2 PxP** (the threat was . . . P–B5), **RxP; 3 B–N3, BxB; 4 RPxB, R–N1**—there is no rush to capture the Pawn; Black prefers to seize an open file first.

(155) SHAFFER—EVANS, U.S. OPEN CHAMPIONSHIP, 1949. (See Diagrams 44, 45, 46.)

1 . . . P–Q4—on the principle of repairing the backward QP (also involved is the pin motif). Black's QP is backward on an open file *temporarily*. Note that it has no Pawn on an adjacent file *behind* it (refer to definition—Diagram 36). The game continued: **2 BPxP, PxP; 3 KR–Q1, PxP; 4 P–B4, R–Q2; 5 RxR, NxR; 6 R–Q1, Q–B3; 7 K–B2, P–QN4; 8 Q–N3, N–N3; 9 P–R3, N–B5** with a winning position.

(156) HEARST—EVANS, MARSHALL CHESS CLUB JR. CHAMPIONSHIP, 1947. (See Diagram 15.)

Black has the outside passed Pawn. The game is drawn after **1 . . . P–N6; 2 PxP, PxP; 3 K–B3** (forced), **K–B4; 4 KxP, K–N5; 5 K–B3, K–R6; 6 K–K4, P–R4** (not 6 . . . KxP??; 7 P–N4 followed by P–B5 and White wins!); **7 K–Q3, KxP; 8 K–B2.** The outside passed Pawn is an advantage, but here it is not quite sufficient to force the win. Note that if Black's Pawn were on R4 in the original position, he wins!

(157) JACKSON—EVANS, LOG CABIN CHESS CLUB CHAMPIONSHIP, 1950. (See Diagrams 67, 68.)

1 P–N6! The game continued: **1 . . . BPxP** (forced); **2 NxP** and Black's Pawn Structure is a shambles, though he managed to hold the game—God knows how!

(158) FRENCH DEFENSE PAWN FORMATION. (See Diagrams 62, 63.)

The base to Black's QP is located on KB2. White has weak light squares; Black has weak dark squares. White's QP has no base. White's Structure is slightly inferior, but not if he can get in P–B5.

154

(159) KELLNER—EVANS, U.S. OPEN CHAMPIONSHIP, 1950. (See Diagrams 18, 61.)

Neither is really bad. The question is: which is "better"? This could conceivably be a matter of opinion. I would say that 1 . . . P–Q4 is too static, too inflexible, not to mention the consequent weakening of K4. **1 . . . P–Q3** is more dynamic because it prepares action in the center with P–K4 or P–QB4, possibly bringing the KB to life in the ensuing opening of lines. In such positions the least committal move is generally desirable. Black can always advance with P–Q4 later, but he can never retract the Pawn to Q3. The game continued: **1 . . . P–Q3; 2 P–KR3, QN–Q2; 3 O–O, P–K4; 4 P–K4** (to free the QB), **N–R4; 5 P–Q5, N–B4** and already Black has good play on the dark squares.

(160) HEARST—EVANS, MARSHALL CHESS CLUB JR. CHAMPIONSHIP, 1946. (See Diagrams 54, 60.)

White is weak on his light squares: Q3, K4.

Remember—*sharp ideas*, not isolated moves, are required. This is tough, but based on what you have learned you should be able to dredge up a partial answer. Incidentally, let us dispose of 1 . . . O–O which, though it embodies the principle of rapid development, does not particularly qualify as a *sharp* idea.

   I. The *stolid* **1 . . . N(4)–N3,** which forces White to part with the two Bishops and threatens to win the KP. White is hard-pressed for an adequate reply. If 2 B–Q3, BxB; 3 QxB, NxP. If 2 B–N3, N–B4; 3 B–K3 (not 3 O–O, B–Q6, winning the exchange), N–Q6ch.

  II. The *cunning* **1 . . . Q–B2**—forcing 2 P–B4, thus forcing White to weaken himself still further on the white squares, and the QR2–KN8 diagonal as well. This could be followed up with 2 . . . P–N4.

 III. The *forceful* **1 . . . P–N4,** with the idea of obtaining an immediate bind on the white squares. If 2 B–N3, Q–B2; 3 P–KB4, N–B4. Or if 2 BxN, BPxB! with a powerful outpost on QB5, a bind, and a potential minority attack. (True, QB5 is not technically a "hole," but if White ever tried P–QN3 to drive away a piece stationed there he would create a backward QBP.) If White now continues with 3 QxP, R–QN1 followed by RxP is strong.

(161) EVANS—HANS, MATCH, 1946. (See Diagram 69.)

White has the good Bishop because his Pawns are on dark squares, whereas Black's Bishop is hemmed in by its own Pawns.

(162) HEARST—EVANS, U.S. OPEN CHAMPIONSHIP, 1953. (See Diagram 58.)

With **1 N–B4!** The game continued: **1 . . . Q–Q1; 2 NxN, NxN; 3 BxN!, PxB** (3 . . . QxB?; 4 N–N6, QxQ; 5 PxQ, R–N1; 6 B–B4); **4 N–N6, R–N1; 5 NxB, RxN; 6 RxR, QxR; 7 QxQP,** winning a Pawn.

(163) EVANS—HARROLD, MARSHALL CHESS CLUB CHAMPIONSHIP, 1946–47. (See Diagram 137.)

1 . . . NxN; 2 BxB, QxB; 3 BxN, Q–N5ch; 4 Q–Q2, QxNP; 5 O–O, Q–R6 and Black lives to tell the tale. The principle involved is timely liquidation (or exchange with gain of Time) followed by a fork.

(164) EVANS—REHBERG, MARSHALL CHESS CLUB CHAMPIONSHIP, 1949–50. (See Diagram 106.)

1 P–K6!, PxP (forced); **2 QxPch, R–B2; 3 N–B7, N–B1** (relatively better is 3 . . . Q–B1); **4 RxQ, BxQ; 5 RxR, RxB; 6 NxB,** *Black Resigns.*

(165) EVANS—BILLS, U.S. OPEN CHAMPIONSHIP, 1954. (See Diagram 145.)

1 P–B4, *Black Resigns.* (If 1 . . B–Q3; 2 BxNch.) K–R1; The principles, of course, are pin and discovered attack.

(166) DUNST—EVANS, MARSHALL CHESS CLUB CHAMPIONSHIP, 1946–47. (See Diagram 54.)

1 . . . B–KB4!; 2 Q–K2 (the Queen is "overloaded," like an electric circuit. It cannot defend against Q–Q5ch and guard the Bishop at the same time), **Q–Q5ch; 3 K–R1, QxB.**
If instead **2 Q–Q5, R–B4; 3 Q–R8ch, K–N2; 4 Q–N7ch, R–B2; 5 Q–Q5, R–Q1** threatening **B–B4ch,** poses White an unanswerable problem.

(167) EVANS—LAMBERT, DUBROVNIK OLYMPICS, 1950. (See Diagram 149.)

Because it sets up a masked attack: **1 QxP?, NxKP!** leads to a won game (2 QxN?, R–K1; or if 2 Q–Q3, NxN; 3 PxN, B–B4 followed by R–K1ch).
The game continued: **1 N–K2, R–K1; 2 P–B3, P–B4!; 3 PxPep., PxP; 4 NxP, Q–N3.** Black's strong counterplay on the dark squares eventually netted him his Pawn back and the game ended in a short, but lively, draw.

(168) CROSS—EVANS, U.S. OPEN CHAMPIONSHIP, 1955. (See Diagrams 54, 59.)

1 . . . P–K4!; 2 N–B3, Q–B4ch; 3 K–R1, N–B7ch; 4 RxN, QxR winning the exchange. The game continued: **5 PxP, PxP; 6 NxP, B–K3.**

(169) ULVESTAD—EVANS, HOLLYWOOD OPEN, 1954. (See Diagram 60.)

On the dark squares (QR3, QN2, QB3, Q4, K3, KB4, KN3, KR5).
Black must penetrate on them. He must demolish the blockade on White's QR4 then invade on the KR file. 1 . . . R–KR1 will not do because of N–R5. The game continued: **1 . . . N–R1!!; 2 Q–K2** (2 K–N2 is slightly better, but White is quite lost in any event), **N–N3; 3 NxN, Q–B6!** (a slight interpolation); **4 NxB, KxN; 5 R–R2, QxNch; 6 K–B1, R–KR1** followed by a fatal penetration on the KR file. White's Bishop is lifeless. He resigned in a few more moves.

(170) EVANS—LECORNU, U.S. OPEN CHAMPIONSHIP, 1952. (See Diagrams 59, 79.)

1 N–K5—on the principles of forcing entry on weak squares and playing to win the "two Bishops."

Black's KP is momentarily backward. If White wants to exploit it, he must try to remove the QB, which is a good defensive piece. The move is tactically justified in view of **1 . . . PxN; 2 PxP, R–Q2; 3 PxB,** conferring White with the two Bishops and an overwhelming Space advantage. The attacker always wants to open lines.
The game continued: **1 . . . Q–K1; 2 NxB, QxN; 3 P–B4, K–R1** (to prevent any harassing pins later on the QR2–KN8 diagonal after Black plays P–K4); **4 R–Q2** followed by R(2)–K2, with a bind.

(171) KASHDAN—EVANS, HOLLYWOOD OPEN, 1954. (See Diagram 147.)

There are two ways for Black to win a Pawn, and he must select that method which allows White least counterplay.

    I. **1 . . . PxP; 2 PxP, RxR; 3 NxR** (forced), **NxKP; 4 QxN, B–B4; 5 Q–R4, BxN**—but this is not so good because of **6 B–N5** (6 . . . P–B3; 7 RxB, PxB; 8 NxP).

    II. The game continued: **1 . . . P–N5; 2 N–K2, NxKP; 3 QxN, B–B4; 4 Q–R4, BxR; 5 B–N5, BxP; 6 BxP, Q–Q2; 7 N–N5, P–R3; 8 N–K4, P–N4; 9 BxP, PxB; 10 NxNP, B–B3,** with adequate defenses to weather the attack and win by sheer preponderance of Force.

(172) EVANS—HESSE, U.S. CHAMPIONSHIP, 1948. (See Diagram 135.)

If **1 P–K4?, PxP; 2 PxP, NxP; 3 QxN?, R–K1** wins the Queen.
White is behind in development and Time. He has the two Bishops and should try to harvest them slowly, either by 1 B–N5 or P–K3, which was played in the game, with the idea of slowly building up P–K4 after castling and placing the Rooks on central files.

(173) EVANS—R. BYRNE, U.S. OPEN CHAMPIONSHIP, 1946. (See Diagram 112.)

Black has a bind on the dark squares. White is saddled with the bad Bishop. The immediate threat is **1 . . . N–K5.** White tried to obtain counterplay by sacrificing the exchange with **1 RxP, RxR; 2 QxN,** but too late—Black's advantage in Force proved decisive. The best defense would have been 1Q–K3.

(174) EVANS—RESHEVSKY, U.S. OPEN CHAMPIONSHIP, 1955. (See Diagram 107.)

Black should recapture with the Pawn so as to free his QB. **1 . . . NxP; 2 P–K4** gains White a tempo; after **1 . . . QxP; 2 N–B3, B–N5; 3 B–Q2** Black must either lose a tempo moving his Queen or give up the two Bishops with BxN. In either event, he still has to solve the problem of freeing his QB.

(175) GASSEN—EVANS, MARSHALL CHESS CLUB CHAMPIONSHIP PRELIMS. (See Diagram 41.)

White's Pawns on Q4 and QB4 are known technically as "hanging Pawns." They are in a state of flux—mobile and not mobile at the same time. Here White's QBP is a target—

and Black should play against it on the principle of piling up on targets.

The game continued: **1 . . . N–QR4; 2 N–K5** (forced), **BxB; 3 KxB, Q–R3** followed by QR–B1, putting more pressure on White's weak point.

(176) PILNICK—EVANS, U.S. OPEN CHAMPIONSHIP, 1952. (See Diagram 37.)

White is tied down to the defense of his backward QBP. Black controls the QB file and has an unassailable outpost on QB5.

(177) EVANS—LARSEN, U.S. OPEN CHAMPIONSHIP, 1949. (See Diagram 23.)

With **1 R–R2!**—followed by R–K2 and P–K4, setting up the steamroller.

(178) EVANS—CARLYLE, U.S. OPEN CHAMPIONSHIP, 1952. (See Diagram 22.)

With **1 P–B3!** Against this Dutch Defense formation White must prepare to break through in the center with P–K4. Black's backward KP will eventually be exposed to an open K-file. The game continued: **1 . . . Q–K1; 2 P–K4, N–Q2; 3 KPxQP, KPxP; 4 B–B4, N–K3; 5 PxP, NxB; 6 NxN,** winning a Pawn.

(179) EVANS—MACCIONI, DUBROVNIK OLYMPICS, 1950. (See Diagrams 22, 23.)

Anyone in his right senses can see that Black controls his K5 four times and White only three times, and that therefore P–K4 is quite unplayable.

However, in this instance wrong senses are needed. **P–K4** is playable because of tactics. The game continued; **1 P–K4!, PxP; 2 PxP, BxKP; 3 RxN!, BxB; 4 RxB!** (the Rook "sells his life as dearly as possible" is the quaint way Nimzo-vitch would phrase it; Euwe calls this a "desperado" theme), **QxR; 5 KxB,** and White has won two pieces for a Rook and Pawn—the game is still difficult, but he has a winning advantage.

(180) EVANS—MARRO, MARSHALL CHESS CLUB JR. CHAMPIONSHIP, 1947. (See Diagram 42.)

He most certainly should! Black's KP is backward, and if White does not capture now there will be no way to get at it.

The game continued: **1 PxPep., BxP; 2 P-B4** (to prevent P-K4), **P-QR4; 3 B-KR3, N-B2; 4 N(2)-B3,** with a bind.

(181) EVANS—HUDSON, INTERCOLLEGIATE TEAM TOURNAMENT, 1950. (See Diagram 108.)

Black's last move does not exert enough pressure on White's center—especially on the crucial K4 square. Better was ... B-N5 (instead of ... P-N3.) The game continued: **1 P-K4, B-N2; 2 P-B3, P-Q3; 3 KN-K2, QN-Q2; 4 B-K3, B-K2; 5 P-KN3, P-K4; 6 P-Q5** with a Space advantage.

(182) EVANS—MEDNIS, U.S. OPEN CHAMPIONSHIP, 1954. (See Diagram 141.)

If White regained his Pawn with the prosaic **1 QxP,** then Black would have time to consolidate with **1 ... P-N3.**
1 P-N6!, however, completely shatters Black's game. Play continued: **1 ... PxP** (forced); **2 NxP, Q-N1; 3 NxR,** winning the exchange.

(183) HANS—EVANS, MATCH, 1946. (See Diagram 108.)

The Queen's Indian Defense is a fight for control of White's K4 square. If **1 O-O,** then N-K5 followed by P-KB4 and Black claims squatter's rights. Therefore, the most accurate move is **1 Q-B2,** on the principle of restriction.

(184) BURGER—EVANS, U.S. OPEN CHAMPIONSHIP, 1952. (See Diagrams 79, 80, 81.)

1 ... B-B1!—on the principle of preserving the two Bishops. Give yourself only half credit if you said **1 ... B-R3.** For after **2 B-K3** Black still is faced with the original problem. The game continued: **2 N-K3, B-K3; 3 P-R5, P-B4; 4 P-KN3, B-R3; 5 R-K2, P-B5; 6 PxP, BxP** and White was slowly ground to death.

(185) FINK—EVANS, U.S. OPEN CHAMPIONSHIP, 1953. (See Diagram 111.)

1 ... P-QR4 secures the advanced outpost by preventing P-QN4; however, it gives White time to get in P-K4. No, **1 ... P-K5!** must be played, if only for its nuisance value! True, Black weakens his Pawn Structure by voluntarily creating an artificially isolated Pawn—but this is a strong cramping influence, a thorn in White's center.
The game continued: **2 N-K1** (2 N-Q2, R-K1; 3 P-QN4, N-Q6 is good for Black), **P-QR4** (now Black has time to do

this); **3 N–R4, NxN; 4 BxN, N–N5; 5 P–KR3, N–K4;
6 Q–K2, Q–R5; 7 B–Q1, P–R4** with a fierce attack.

In other words, it is more important for Black to restrain
White from consolidating his center than to secure his
advanced outpost (Black Knight on QB4). This is a problem
of evaluation and calculation. Before Black pushes his Pawn
to K5, he must be assured that White cannot win it.

CHAPTER SEVEN: New Approach to the Openings

Diagram 186

"A complicated position"—Breyer

Evaluation

By "evaluation" is meant recognition of the various criteria which determine the advantage in a given position at a given moment, and then weighing them against each other to ascertain which side has that advantage. The original position at the start of each game is symmetrical. With "best play" (whatever that is) the "perfect game of chess" (whatever that is) should conclude in a draw. This statement is more an ethical demand than a mathematical certainty. Emanuel Lasker wrote: "Balanced positions with best play on either side must lead again and again to balanced positions." However, there is no real "balance" in chess because it is a dynamic game; positions are continually in flux; one move may completely alter the outcome. If we describe chess in terms of Force (F), Space (S), Time (T), and Pawn Structure (P), then Lasker's axiom may be expressed mathematically (where F′, S′, T′, P′ describe Black) thus:

$$\frac{F + S + T + P}{F' + S' + T' + P'} = 1$$

In other words, where neither side has an advantage in Force, Space, Time, or Pawn Structure, the probable outcome is a draw. From this it follows that the question of a win arises only after one player holds an uncompensated advantage in any one of these elements.

Steinitz was the first chess philosopher who sought to govern his own play by this equation. In the words of Lasker: "Steinitz elevates himself to the level of a genuine philosopher in demanding that the player (with an advantage) *must* attack with intent to win or else be punished by being deprived of his advantage." From this it follows that the converse also holds: that a player who seeks to win without first having an advantage should be prepared to pay the ultimate penalty—namely, defeat.

Steinitz had the self-discipline and the objectivity to evaluate each position as though he himself were not personally involved. He realized, of course, that the chessmaster must have a "killer instinct"; but he also perceived that the mere will-to-win was not enough to bring about victory. In this respect, Botvinnik more resembles Steinitz in temperament than any other world champion. Alekhine's games, on the other hand, are characterized by sheer will, the fierce attempt to exert mind over matter.

RUBINSTEIN—LASKER, ST. PETERSBURG, 1909

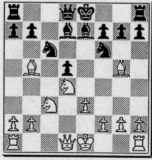

Diagram 187

163

White to move—Force or Time? *Most masters today probably would choose Time and play* 10 O–O *in order to complete development and maintain slow, steady pressure against Black's isolated QP. Not Rubinstein. He plays to win the QP immediately, even though he must submit to an apparently irresistible attack in order to do so. The attack is so dangerous that players noted for their boldness would probably abstain—rightly so, perhaps. Rubinstein himself had frequently rejected sacrifices of this sort and continued instead with quiet positional chess. Here the attack on Black's QP is the motif. If White doesn't capture it now, he never will: e.g.,* 10 O–O, NxN; 11 BxBch, QxB; 12 QxN, P–KR3; 13 B–R4 *(not* 13 BxN, BxB; 14 QxQP?, BxNch, *winning the Queen),* O–O; 14 O–O, KR–Q1; 15 KR–Q1, Q–K3—*White has a superior game, but no win of a Pawn in sight.*

According to Réti (in *Masters of the Chessboard*) if Rubinstein failed to take the Pawn, he would cease to heed that inner ethical voice, cease to be that humble and submissive player who trusted in his own judgment—which tells him that despite the danger he can take the Pawn and get away with it—that if he does not exercise his advantage now, it will evaporate. In the end Rubinstein did take the Pawn—with fear and trembling, to be sure—but confident that what is right must prevail.

WHITE	BLACK	WHITE	BLACK
10 BxKN	BxB	16 R–B1!	RxN[5]
11 NxP	BxN	17 RxBch!	PxR
12 PxB	Q–N4[1]	18 Q–B1!![6]	RxP
13 BxN	BxB	19 PxR!	R–Q2[7]
14 N–K3[2]	O–O–O[3]	20 QxPch	K–Q1
15 O–O	KR–K1[4]	21 R–B4![8]	

[1] Rubinstein now abstains from 13 N–B7ch, K–Q1; 14 NxR, QxB —and Black wins. Both players were now relying on intuition, as it was impossible to calculate the ensuing complications with absolute precision.

On whose side is justice: the materialist (Rubinstein) or the idealist (Lasker)?

The double threat against Q5 and N2 forces 13 BxN, which leaves Black with superb development as compensation for his Pawn minus. Incidentally, no good was 12 . . . Q–R4ch instead of the text because of 13 Q–Q2, and if QxB?; 14 N–B7ch, winning the Queen by a fork.

[2] Not 14 N–B7ch, K–Q2; 15 NxR, R–K1ch.

[3] Plausible, but insufficient. Relatively better is 14 . . . BxP; 15 NxB (if 15 R–KN1, Q–R4ch), QxN; 16 Q–K2ch, K–Q1; 17 O–O–O —White has excellent attacking chances, and this is the reason Lasker rejects the gain of a Pawn.

[4] It begins to look as if White must pay the piper. If now 16 P–KN3 (to meet the threat of RxN), then Black's attack gains irresistible momentum with RxN!; 17 PxR, QxKPch; 18 R–B2, Q–K5. Rubinstein rubs his eyes. He cannot believe that White is lost merely because he followed the dictates of the position. A humble believer in "justice," he seeks salvation in the form of a miracle.

[5] Forced. If 16 . . . K–N1; 17 R–B5!, Q–N3; 18 P–Q5, retaining the extra Pawn and beating back the attacking forces.

[6] This is the miracle! Through this move—and only this move— White keeps his extra Pawn and nurses it through to an endgame which is handled with chiselled perfection.

[7] The lesser evil. If 19 . . . R–Q3; 20 RxP.

[8] White succeeded in exchanging Queens and winning the Rook and Pawn ending. If now 21 . . . R–Q8ch; 22 K–B2, R–Q7ch; 23 K–B1!, R–Q8ch; 24 K–K2. The previous sequence is a fine example of utilizing Time to simplify, and thereby to maintain Force (the extra Pawn).

Is the First Move an Advantage?

Under the above heading, W. F. Streeter wrote an article in the May, 1946 *Chess Review* in which he summarized the results by color of 5,598 games played between 1851–1932 in 45 tournaments. His conclusions follow:

1851–1878—White won 46%, Black won 40%, Drawn 14%
1881–1914—White won 37%, Black won 31%, Drawn 32%
1914–1932—White won 37%, Black won 26%, Drawn 37%
Total   —*White won* 38%, *Black won* 31%, *Drawn* 31%

It thus appears that it is becoming increasingly difficult to win with the Black pieces, but somewhat easier to draw. Some of us may refuse to be tyrannized by these statistics. We may argue, the results of these games had nothing to do with who moved first. The better player will win regardless of which color he has. Since we must assume that the strong players had Black as often as White, we can only infer that White won more games because of the advantage of the first move. This advantage (however slight) does confer White the initiative.

Master Practice

The way in which theoreticians evaluate a given opening variation is to examine the outcomes of master games in which this opening is adopted. However, results are deceptive because the outcome does not necessarily reflect which side had the better of it after a given number of moves. A stronger player may be handling the theoretically inferior position and win by virtue of his ability; any number of blunders or time-pressure errors may also intervene—not to mention the classic domestic battle of "the night before." The basic trouble is that evaluations are static while a game is dynamic; and this casts serious doubt on the traditional criterion of evaluation —namely, master practice.

The Failure of Traditional Evaluation

If we pick up a copy of *Modern Chess Openings* we will find these symbols accompanied by these explanations.

  ++after White (or Black's move); White (Black) has a winning advantage.

  +after White (or Black's move): White (Black) has a distinct superiority, but there is no forced win.

  ±White stands slightly better.

  ∓Black stands slightly better.

  =The position offers equal chances.

These well known symbols have been used by nearly every theoretician in the chess world in order to evaluate a given position. The soundness of the evaluation depends upon the playing strength of the theoretician who is assigning the valuation, and he is almost never a Grandmaster.

Let us examine a specific position, discuss the traditional approach, then apply our new method.

Diagram 188

White to move—who stands better? This position was thought to be equal until 1954, when Geller found a new move for White. The first thing we notice is that it is White's move. He has the initiative. True, **1 RxN** is impossible because of **R–Q8 mate.** The question is whether White has a way to prevent Black from retreating his Knight to Q3 or B3, followed by consolidation, with a draw as the likely outcome. One thing is clear: White must exploit his Time advantage or lose it. If White can clear his last rank (*by moving his Q-Bishop with a gain of tempo*), then he can safely play RxN. Geller's sharp move, **1 B–R6!** fits this prescription. The last rank has been cleared and the gain of tempo is accomplished by the attack on Black's KNP. If now **1 . . . PxB; 2 RxN,** and White has a winning endgame advantage (*formula:* Initiative *translated into better* Pawn Structure).

The tactical justification of **1 B–R6** lies in two possibilities with Black's "desperado" Knight. (A "desperado" is a piece which must be lost anyway, and in exchange for which one therefore tries to get as much compensation as possible.)

First possibility: **1 . . . NxQBP; 2 BxP, KR–N1; 3 NxP!, KxN** (not **3 . . . RxB; 4 NxR, KxN; 5 PxN,** winning the exchange); **4 BxN,** and White has won a Pawn (formula: *Initiative* translated into superior *Force*).

At this point the chess world condemned this position for Black, and therefore the moves leading up to it had to be abandoned. Just to illustrate the difficulty of pinning anything down to a final evaluation, it now appears, upon re-examination, that Black does have a tactical saving clause.

Second possibility: **1 . . . NxKBP!; 2 BxP** (if **2 B–B4, N–Q6; 3 NxN, RxN; 4 BxP, K–Q2**—draw), **KR–N1; 3 B–B6!, N–R6ch; 4 K–B1, BxB; 5 N–N4 dis. ch, K–B1!** (not **5 . . . B–K2; 6 N–B6ch, K–B1; 7 NxR,** winning); **6 NxB, R–N3; 7 NxPch, K–N2; 8 PxN, KxN** and Black should be able to draw the Rook and Pawn ending since White's extra Pawn is doubled and therefore negligible.

So now—where are we? Back where we started perhaps? Not exactly. Unless a further improvement is found for White, the original evaluation of "equality" must be restored (=). Or perhaps we might assign White a slight edge ($\pm$). Geller's innovation is strong but apparently not decisive. There is no way for White to convert his advantage in Time into a forced win. Yet how much richer is chess theory for our having plumbed this position to its depths!

Although enriched, we are still unable to retire. We are no nearer the answers to two questions: (1) how are evaluations arrived at in the first place? (2) is there any *method* of arriving at one which is "self-contained," i.e., states the premises from which it is derived?

Our discussion of the previous positions provides us with a lead. We referred to three elements: *Time* ("initiative" is a sub-heading), *Force, Pawn Structure.* (Neither side has a marked advantage in *Space*.) From this it follows that *all positions may be broken down into their component elements, then evaluated accordingly.*

The concept which the theoretician accords primacy is practice, or past master experience with a given position. There is no way to divorce theory from practice. We can't say, for instance, that White stands better here even though he has lost every tournament game continuing from this position. If that's the case, then there is something wrong with our original evaluation.

The function of the chess critic is to provide a court of last resort. However, critics have been guilty of the subjective fallacy: they have permitted names, reputations, and the outcome of doubtful games to influence their evaluation of opening variations. Taking a case at random, let us again turn to *Modern Chess Openings* (8th edition)— column 15 in the Slav Defense: Alekhine's opinion is quoted—thus evidently sanctioned—that "Black stands slightly better."

Diagram 189

White to move—who stands better? *This question can be approached only by breaking down this position into its component parts and then weighing an advantage in one element against a disadvantage in another, finally arriving at a conclusion. (This "weighing" is where a master's opinion is required.)*

Force: Material is equal. White has the two Bishops: an edge.

Space: White has the freer game. True, Black's pieces strike at 12 squares beyond the frontier line and White's pieces at only 11—yet the fact that it is White's move is worth several squares. **1 P–R5,** for instance, would cramp Black.

Time: Each side has three pieces developed and is ready to castle in one move. However, it is White's move. He has the initiative.

Pawn Structure: Black has doubled Pawns. White has two possible points of breakthrough: K4 or/and QR6. He can force an immediate breach in Black's Q-side Pawns by P–QR5–6.

Practice: None quoted.

Hence we conclude that White stands better in every possible way, that Black has no counter-vailing resources. This evaluation is positive and irrefutable. That is not to say that Black will not win this game (of course he can), only that he should avoid this particular position because other ones with the same variation (in the Slav Defense) give him better chances.

Of course, most conclusions are not so clear-cut. The gambit, for instance, involves the problem of weighing Force against Time and Space. The K-side gambits have been analyzed to such a point of exhaustion that theory can provide a court of last resort without fearing the wrath of time. Take the Evans Gambit. Theory decrees that White has insufficient compensation for the Pawn. This is true now and should also be true one hundred years from now despite the "light of later developments." Let us see why. Our conclusion will be that *Force plus Pawn Structure vs. Space and Time.*

THE EVANS GAMBIT

Diagram 190

Force: If all other things were equal (which they are not), Black's extra Pawn would be decisive. It is in this element that Black's main advantage lies.

Space: Black leads 6 to 5, but White will have an advantage after the inevitable expansion with P–Q4. White's QN is deprived of its best square on QB3. White's Bishop controls a more important diagonal than Black's.

169

Time: White has the move and the initiative. He can develop quick threats by Q–N3 coupled with P–Q4. White can castle in one move. Black will have trouble bringing his King to safety.

Pawn Structure: This is Black's long-range trump card! If and when he returns the Pawn, he will still have the better endgame structure (this is the theme of Lasker's Defense). Black has absolutely no organic weaknesses, whereas White has inflicted a critical gash in his Q-side by playing P–QN4. The endgame is permanently in Black's favor—if he can ever get to it.

Practice: (Here the book would quote games.) Black's defense has proven so adequate that White has virtually abandoned the Evans Gambit. Black has violated no basic principles by developing his Knight and Bishop, therefore he need fear no diversionary tactics on the part of his opponent so early in the game.

While White has *some* compensation for the sacrificed Pawn, it is not sufficient. Hence the case is closed on the Evans Gambit. A Grandmaster will essay it against an equal player only *if*: (*a*) he has an improvement up his sleeve; (*b*) he knows it is inferior but counts on his familiarity with it and the element of surprise; (*c*) he rejects the entire matrix from which traditional evaluation is launched. Of these three, "*b*" is most likely.

Incidentally, the meaning of "equality" solves itself when we evaluate in this manner. *Evaluation is not a prediction of result.* It is merely an attempt to weigh dynamic elements at a given moment. An equal sign (=) states that *in the opinion of the editor* neither side holds an uncompensated advantage. Equality does not mean that the game *should* be drawn, merely that the *winning chances* available to both sides are in a state of dynamic balance. Between masters an advantage in the opening is often crucial, despite Alekhine's boast that to lose a game he had to be beaten three times—once in the opening, once in the middle game, and once in the ending.

A Self-contained Evaluation

Obviously, an exhaustive analysis such as we undertook on the previous positions could not be applied to an opening encyclopedia, crammed with variations, because of the space and expense involved. Yet it is clearly desirable that an evaluation contain the reasoning wherewith it is derived. The only solution lies in the use of increased symbolization. In this fashion, the last evaluation on the Evans Gambit may be expressed:

$$FP \mp - ST$$

This is read: "Force and Pawn Structure [FP] are in Black's favor [∓]. White has some compensation in Space and Time [ST]."

Admittedly, symbolization and other technical jargon are always irksome to the layman. But a player seeking reference books for enlightenment is not likely to be refreshed by literary grace. Besides, he can always ignore the editor's evaluation and draw his own conclusions anyway. Symbols, once standardized, are universal in nature. They would doubtlessly save blobs of ink and thousands of wasted words. Such a task might be solved some day by the use of a computer.

The First Move

If we approach the opening without prejudice, then there are some few but important truths which may be taken for granted. We know that the center is of paramount importance, that pieces must somehow be developed, and that too many Pawn moves create weaknesses. This is the starting point.

A glance at the original position reveals 20 possible opening moves—16 with the Pawns and 4 with the Knights. Which of these is best—and why—no one knows. "It is astonishing how much hot water a master can wade into in the first dozen moves, despite a century of opening exploration" (Napier). The choice of a first move narrows down to individual style, for chess is one of the last remaining realms of free will.

As I write, I am looking at the board with a completely open mind. It occurs to me that of these 20 moves, perhaps only 3 are perfectly horrible: P–QR4, P–KR4, P–KN4—they create gaping weaknesses in the Pawn Structure, contribute nothing toward development, contain no threat, and make no contest for control of the center. Yet at the New York Tournament, 1880, Ware played 1 . . . P–QR4 every time he had Black—winning four and losing five. With White, he also began two games with 1 P–QR4—winning one and losing the other.

Two apparently useless Knight moves—N–KR3 and N–QR3—may be espoused by some Réti of the future who will give them a double exclamation mark in ultra-modern fashion. To the modern master, who has been bred with the principle of mobility, these moves seem outlandish and anti-positional. Yet no doubt they will appear in chess of the future (*circa* 2000) because the moves which are today considered normal will have been so exhaustively analyzed. There is a real possibility that chess openings will be played-out and that in future tournaments players will draw cards to select the opening which shall be played (as in checkers today). Perhaps this all sounds facetious. Yet as early as 1868, at London, a tournament already was contested wherein all the participants began their games with the positions of their Knights and Bishops reversed—to avoid book-play and to throw the players on their own resources. This is reminiscent of the optimistic proposal in the late nineteenth century that the United States close its patent bureau on the grounds that everything worthwhile had already been invented!

Right now there is a lot of scope in the chess openings, and a lot of room for discovery and innovation. Very few masters have conquered all the intricacies of *even one* variation. At the 1933 Folkestone Team Tournament, Arthur Dake defeated Hans Muller, the writer of an authoritative treatise on the English Opening, in 21 moves. The opening was an *English Opening*!

Reverse Openings

Both 1 P–Q4 and 1 P–K3 free two pieces and contest the center— such is the motive behind them. *Yet the moment any Pawn advances two squares it creates an irretrievable weakness and provides a natural target.* Once White has committed himself, Black is the master of which course the defense shall take. This is the reason many a player who excels at counter attack wins more games with the Black pieces than with White. Black's defenses are so good, in fact, that they must be even better for White if he plays them with a move-in-hand.

The logical choice for these "reverse openings" is the K's Indian formation. It has proved itself a resilient and successful weapon for the second player, and, curiously enough, there is no way to prevent White from setting it up. Thus, a player needs familiarize himself thoroughly with only one variation *regardless of what Black replies.*

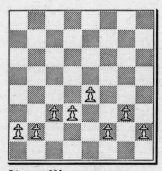

Diagram 191

The K's Indian Pawn Structure

This basic structure is also common to the Pirc Defense (1 P–K4, P–Q3), Philidor's Defense (1 P–K4, P–K4; 2 N–KB3, P–Q3). White's position contains a weakness at Q3, but this is offset by his ability to maneuver behind the lines. The weak white square complex (KB3 and KR3) is negligible as long as the K-Bishop is retained. In some cases the QRP advances to QR4 in order to defend an advanced Knight outpost at QB4 (so that it cannot be dislodged by . . . P–QN4).

After 1 P–K4 or 1 N–KB3 White can force the game into channels of his own choosing against any defense. Thus, against the French (1 P–K4, P–K3) 2 P–Q3 produces the desired result.

Diagram 192

The French Defense—after 2 P–Q3

The game might continue: **2 . . . P–Q4; 3 N–Q2, N–KB3; 4 P–KN3, B–K2; 5 B–N2, O–O; 6 KN–B3, P–B4; 7 O–O, N–B3**—all logical moves.

Diagram 193

Position after 7 . . . N–B3

173

Notice how exactly the same position may be reached by transposition, as in the game Evans—Sherwin, Rosenwald Tourney, N.Y., 1954–55: **1 N–KB3, N–KB3; 2 P–KN3, P–Q4; 3 B–N2, P–K3; 4 O–O, B–K2; 5 P–Q3** (White just closes his eyes, oblivious to Black's contortions), **O–O; 6 QN–Q2, P–B4; 7 P–K4, N–B3.** *Voilà!*

In this example Black had option. He could have imitated White's moves, since he had not already committed himself with 1 . . . P–K3 on his very first move as in the French Defense.

To show how quickly White can whip up an attack, follow the Evans—Sherwin continuation from the diagram: **8 P–B3, R–N1; 9 R–K1, R–K1; 10 P–K5, N–Q2; 11 N–B1, P–QN4; 12 P–KR4!, P–QR4** (initiating an attack on the opposite wing); **13 B–B4, B–QR3; 14 N(1)–R2, Q–B2; 15 P–R5, P–N5; 16 N–N4, P–R5; 17 P–B4, PxP; 18 PxP, BxP; 19 QxP, N–N3; 20 Q–B2, P–N6; 21 PxP, N–N5; 22 Q–B3, N(5)–Q4; 23 Q–B1, BxP; 24 B–N5, N–N5; 25 R–K3!, B–Q4; 26 P–R6, P–N3; 27 KR–R3, N–B5; 28 BxB, RxB; 29 Q–B4** with a won game.

It is apparent that there is much attacking potential concealed in White's "passive" formation—especially when Black upsets the balance by seizing the center with Pawns.

With this closed formation the possibilities of transposition are abundant. Reshevsky—Botvinnik, Match U.S. vs. U.S.S.R., Moscow, 1955 continued: **1 P–K4, P–K3; 2 P–Q3, P–QB4!; 3 P–KN3, N–QB3; 4 B–N2, P–KN3; 5 N–Q2, B–N2; 6 KN–B3, KN–K2; 7 O–O, O–O; 8 R–K1, P–Q3; 9 P–B3, P–KR3; 10 N–N3, P–K4; 11 P–Q4, P–N3** and Black, if anything, has the better of it due to the constant threat of P–KB4. This illustrates the danger of White's closing his eyes and playing the system automatically, instead of varying his tactics to meet Black's reply. In this case 5 N–Q2 fails to meet the challenge of the position. White might try instead 5 P–KR4!? which is designed to take advantage momentarily of Black's weak dark square complex. In this respect chess theory undergoes a creative evolution: it requires more sophisticated ideas to combat more sophisticated antidotes.

The Reshevsky—Botvinnik game can also be arrived at via the following plausible order of moves in the Sicilian Defense: **1 P–K4, P–QB4; 2 N–KB3, P–Q3; 3 P–Q3** (the customary move is 3 P–Q4), **N–QB3; 4 P–KN3, P–KN3; 5 B–N2, B–N2; 6 O–O, P–K3** (better immediately is 6 . . . P–K4!—a sophisticated reason why White cannot enter the above game by this side-path); **7 QN–Q2, KN–K2; 8 R–K1, O–O; 9 P–B3, P–KR3; 10 N–N3, P–K4; 11 P–Q4, P–N3** and this position is identical with the one reached above.

The element of Time is not so crucial in closed positions as in open ones. It therefore follows that by adopting the reverse formation

White is avoiding a sharp, early struggle, and postponing the battle until the mid-game. The reason "reverse openings" have lost favor is that White's advantage is too minute, and the game assumes a drawish character when Black maintains the symmetry by copying White's moves.

The Theory of Symmetrical Positions

The original position is symmetrical, and by making his opening move White disturbs the balance. Black can copy—but not for long. For example: **1 P–K4, P–K4; 2 N–KB3, N–KB3** (Petrov's Defense); **3 NxP, NxP?** (correct is 3 . . . P–Q3; 4 N–KB3, NxP); **4 Q–K2, P–Q4; 5 P–Q3** winning a piece, for if 5 . . . N–KB3; 6 N–B6 dis. ch. wins Black's Queen.

In reverse openings, however, Black can copy for a long time, e.g., Evans—Lombardy, N.Y. Met League Championship, 1956: **1 N–KB3, N–KB3** (1 . . . P–Q4—or any Pawn move for that matter —would disturb the symmetry); **2 P–KN3, P–KN3; 3 B–N2, B–N2; 4 O–O, O–O; 5 P–Q3, P–Q3; 6 P–B4, P–B4; 7 N–B3, N–B3; 8 B–Q2** (more accurate is 8 R–N1! and Black cannot copy for long: e.g., 8 . . . R–N1; 9 P–QR3, P–QR3; 10 P–QN4, P–QN4?; 11 PxNP, RPxP; 12 PxP, PxP; 13 RxP winning a Pawn), **R–N1; 9 P–QR3, P–QR3; 10 R–N1, P–QN4** (Black has gained the initiative because of White's faulty 8th move); **11 PxP, PxP; 12 P–QN4, PxP; 13 PxP, B–Q2** (Black rejects either P–K4 or P–Q4, preferring to force White to commit himself first); **14 P–R3, P–R3.**

Diagram 194

Position after 14 . . . P–R3—symmetry

Here we encounter our old axiom: $\dfrac{F' + S' + T' + P'}{F + S + T + P} = 1.$

White has the move (T), but is it really an advantage? In billiards it would not be, for he would have to "crack" the formation and open up lines for his opponent. White must finally commit himself. On 15 P–Q4 Black has the pleasant alternatives of either P–K4 or B–B4. After 15 P–K3, P–K4, Black has achieved the more aggressive center formation, and if now 16 P–K4 (to prevent P–Q4), then it is Black who has gained the move!

Each side is reluctant to disrupt the balance, perhaps remembering the checker maxim that he who disturbs his position the least, disturbs his opponent the most. But White must do something!

If White has an advantage, it is indeed very slight, and the course of the game bears out the axiom: **15 P–K4, N–K1** (Black can copy only to his disadvantage: 15 . . . P–K4; 16 B–K3, B–K3; 17 P–Q4 with the freer position); **16 N–Q5, N–B2; 17 NxN, QxN; 18 P–Q4, P–K4** (inferior is 18 . . . NxP; 19 NxN, BxN; 20 BxP, B–N2; 21 BxB, KxB; 22 Q–Q4ch, K–N1; 23 QR–B1 and White controls all the open lines); **19 Q–B1, Q–B1; 20 BxP, NxQP; 21 NxN, QxQ; 22 BxQ, PxN; 23 R–Q1, KR–B1; 24 B–N2, R–B5; 25 B–QR1,** (threatening B–B1), **B–QB3!; 26 P–B3, P–Q4; 27 B–B1, R–B7; 28 BxQP, PxP; 29 BxQP, PxP; 30 QR–B1, RxR; 31 RxR, R–N3; 32 PxP, BxP; 33 R–B5, B–B3** and the game was shortly drawn.

The symmetrical defense to the Queen's Gambit puts it to its most severe test—up to now no method has been demonstrated that "preserves" White's advantage! **1 P–Q4, P–Q4; 2 P–QB4, P–QB4.**

Diagram 195

Position after 2 . . . P–QB4

The nearest that White has come to holding on to the initiative is with **3 PxQP, N–KB3; 4 N–KB3** (PxP, QxP leads to nothing for White), **PxP; 5 QxP, QxP; 6 N–B3, QxQ; 7 NxQ** followed by P–KN3 and B–N2 with pressure. However, in Evans—Bisguier, Triangular Match, N.Y., 1955, Black continued with 6 . . . Q–QR4 followed by N–B3, regaining the lost tempo—and White could get nothing out of the opening.

176

The only reason this symmetrical defense is not played more often is that it leads to drawish positions—and Black is not content with a draw—even though he is the theoretical underdog!

In the hands of a master technician the advantage of the move is often decisive in many symmetrical positions—witness the following mirror image, from Reshevsky—Ståhlberg, Match, New York vs. Argentina, 1947. White seems to make something out of nothing.

Diagram 196

White moves.

1 B–N5!	R–K1

In order to avoid weaknesses. If 1 . . . P–B3; 2 B–B4 followed by QR–B1 with a bind. Of course not 1 . . . P–K4?; 2 B–K7 winning the exchange. The text is an almost imperceptible error.

The most crucial variation occurs if Black attempts to maintain the symmetry with 1 . . . B–N5; 2 BxP, BxP; 3 BxN, BxN; 4 BxR, BxR; 5 BxB, BxB; 6 KxB, KxB; 7 R–QB1 followed by R–B1 with a bind—but a win is still far from sight.

After 1 . . . B–N5; 2 P–B3, P–B3, there does not seem any way for White to capitalize on his first move.

After the text Black drifts into a lost game without making any further errors.

2 QR–B1	P–KR3
3 B–K3	. . .

The Bishops rake Black's Q-side.

3 . . .	B–B4
4 R–B7	BxN

This seems wrong on principle, but what else can Black do? If 4 . . . QR–B1; 5 KR–B1, RxR; 6 RxR, R–QB1; 7 RxR, BxR; 8 BxQRP and wins.

5 PxB	QR–B1

6 KR–B1	RxR
7 RxR	BxP
8 BxNP	B–B3
9 B–B6	R–N1

Black must lose a Pawn by force, but he can hold out longer after
9 . . . R–QB1; 10 RxR, NxR; 11 BxKRP, N–N3 though White
should still win eventually.

10 BxQRP	R–N8ch
11 K–N2	R–QR8
12 P–QR4	. . .

The march of this Pawn is decisive.   The rest is technique—extremely
instructive.

| 12 . . . | N–B4 |
| 13 B–N6 | . . . |

White carefully shepherds the advance of his RP.

13 . . .	B–Q5
14 P–R5	B–B6
15 R–R7	N–Q5
16 B–K4	N–N6
17 P–R6	B–Q5
18 BxB	NxB
19 R–Q7	P–B4
20 B–Q5ch	*Black Resigns*

CHAPTER EIGHT: Summing Up

THIS book is devoted to the practical question of how the amateur may radically improve his play by applying master principles to his own games. My approach has been to break chess down into its basic components: Pawn Structure, Space, Force, and Time. The order in which they are taken is arbitrary. Pawn structure is considered first because it is the least understood and the most difficult to grasp, even for good players. A realization that the Pawn is the "soul" of chess is prerequisite to further analysis of the other elements.

In chemical terms Pawn Structure and Force are relatively "inert," whereas Space and Time are "volatile." Broadly speaking, an advantage in the inert (or stable) elements manifests itself most decisively in the endgame; an advantage in the volatile (or unstable) elements is most crucial in the opening where rapid development and control of the center are all-important. In the middle game no one element has a tendency to predominate. A decision in the early stages of the game is unlikely between equal players; hence victory is possible only after one has erred. When the minor advantages which accrue are exploited with precision we speak of "technique." Here the problem is to convert the volatile into the inert elements. The bulk of the text deals with practical illustrations taken largely from my own tournament games.

The Stable Elements

Pawn Structure is akin to bone structure. Since the Pawn is the only unit which cannot be retracted once it advances, it should be moved sparingly. Hasty weaknesses can seldom be repaired. The ability of the Pawn to queen when it reaches the eighth rank alters the dynamics of endgame strategy and elevates this "proletariat" to regal significance.

Other things equal, an advantage in Force is decisive. The win of even a single Pawn in the opening usually provides a winning game between equal players. To be ahead in material is to be wealthier than your opponent. He cannot afford to expose the state of his bankruptcy by the constant swapping of pieces. Hence exchanging pieces once you are ahead in material is the pattern for translating Force into victory.

The Unstable Elements

A space advantage means superior mobility, i.e., more elbow room in which to maneuver pieces, fluid lines of communication. Cramped positions bear the germs of defeat. In order to obtain freedom your opponent often will be forced to make grave concessions in Pawn Structure or Force. Then it becomes a question of enforcing that somewhat difficult task of "winning a won game."

An advantage in Time confers the initiative. Pieces which are centralized and well-developed are ready to strike deeply into the heart of enemy terrain. So crucial is tempo that if a player were granted the right to move twice in a row just once every game at his option—while the same right were denied his opponent—he could become world champion.

❋❋❋❋❋❋❋❋❋❋

In Chapter One we reviewed the turmoil between the Romantics, Classicists, Hypermoderns, Technicians and Tacticians. We saw that chess sways between art and science as does Mahomet's coffin between heaven and earth. The game is a competitive struggle between two minds within a mechanistic framework. To Lasker it was a battle of the human personality in which the rounded man and not necessarily the better player was bound to triumph. To Norbert Wiener a machine could be constructed which would probably defeat a "stupid" or "careless" chessplayer, hence "it might very well be as good . . . as the vast majority of the human race."

The American school of chess is bound to be pragmatic because it reflects the culture. The Soviet style is dynamic, based more on counterattack than attack. A noted psychologist has hinted that this style of play mirrors a social structure where individual initiative is reduced to a minimum.

Pragmatism as a method or a way of life becomes obnoxious only when its adherents worship at the fount of success and make the smug deduction that a course of action is "best because it works." The principles advocated here *work because they are best* —there can be no question of subjectivity. They are the distilled heritage of a hundred years of chess evolution. Hypocrisy and error do not survive very long on the chessboard: the merciless fact, culminating in checkmate, contradicts the hypocrite.

✼✼✼✼✼✼✼✼✼

The preceding chapters form an organic whole by showing the valid application of the principles which guide my play as well as that of the other masters both in theory and practice. These are empirical principles derived directly from source-experience: master games. I hope that this book will not only be read, but also referred to many times in the course of your own chess experience. It contains all my "secrets." If someone had set these principles down for me in black and white at the outset of my chess career, he would have saved me perhaps a year of groping in the dark.

The chessboard is a place of joy, stimulation, intellectual challenge. No one knows the divinity who bestowed it upon the world to slay boredom and exhilarate the spirit. Yet chess has travelled without passport, a universal heritage which is the property of all nations. And there is beauty there. . . .

BIBLIOGRAPHY

ALEKHINE, A. *My Best Games of Chess.* In 2 volumes. Harcourt, Brace & Co., New York.

CHERNEV, I. *Winning Chess Traps. Chess Review*, New York, 1946.

DU MONT, J. *The Basis of Combination in Chess.* George Routledge & Sons, Ltd., London, 1946.

EUWE, M. *Meet the Masters.* Sir Isaac Pitman & Sons, Ltd., London, 1945.

EUWE, M. *Strategy and Tactics in Chess.* David McKay Co., Philadelphia, 1937.

EVANS, L. *Trophy Chess.* Charles Scribner & Sons, New York, 1956.

FINE, R. *Basic Chess Endings.* David McKay Co., Philadelphia, 1941.

FINE, R. *The Ideas Behind the Chess Openings.* David McKay, Co., Philadelphia, 1943.

KMOCH, H. *Rubinstein's Chess Masterpieces.* Horowitz & Harkness New York, 1941.

KÖNIG, I. *Chess from Morphy to Botvinnik.* G. Bell & Sons, Ltd., London, 1951.

KORN, W. and EVANS, L. *Modern Chess Openings.* Tenth Edition. Pitman Publishing Corporation, New York, 1965.

LASKER, EM. *Manual of Chess.* David McKay Co., Philadelphia, 1947.

NIMZOVITCH, A. *My System.* David McKay Co., Philadelphia, 1947.

REINFELD, F. *Keres' Best Games of Chess.* David McKay Co., Philadelphia, 1942.

REINFELD, F. *Practical End-Game Play.* David McKay Co., Philadelphia, 1949.

REINFELD, F. *The Immortal Games of Capablanca.* Pitman Publishing Corporation, New York, 1942.

REINFELD, F. & CHERNEV, I. *Chess Strategy and Tactics.* David McKay Co., Philadelphia, 1946.

RÉTI, R. *Masters of the Chessboard.* Whittlesey House, New York.

RÉTI, R. *Modern Ideas in Chess.* David McKay Co., Philadelphia.

SPIELMANN, R. *The Art of Sacrifice in Chess.* David McKay Co., Philadelphia.

ZNOSKO-BOROVSKY, E. *The Middle Game in Chess.* David McKay Co., Philadelphia.

INDEX OF OPPONENTS

(Numbers refer to diagrams)

ADAMS   vs. Evans, 49, 66, 68

ALEKHINE   vs. Réti, 12, 13

AMATEUR   vs. Morphy, 5

ANDERSSEN   vs. Dufresne, 2; Kieseritzky, 1

ASH   vs. Evans, 133

BARDA   vs. Evans, 113

BERLINER   vs. Evans, 89, 152

BILLS   vs. Evans, 165

BISGUIER   vs. Evans, 11, 30, 39, 60; Kashdan, 80; Kramer, 9, 10; Sherwin, 84

BOTVINNIK   vs. Smyslov, 53

BOULACHANIS   vs. Evans, 38

BREYER   vs. Nyholm, 15

BRONSTEIN   vs. Evans, 141

BURGER   vs. Evans, 81, 184

BYRNE, D.   vs. Evans, 110; Reshevsky, 42

BYRNE, R.   vs. Evans, 29, 173

CARLYLE   vs. Evans, 127, 178

COLLINS   vs. Evans, 118, 121

CROSS   vs. Evans, 168

CROSS, J.   vs. Evans, 51

DAKE   vs. Evans, 67

DONOVAN   vs. Evans, 115

DUFRESNE   vs. Anderssen, 2

DUNST   vs. Evans, 166

EUWE   vs. Evans, 32

FINE   vs. Evans, 79

FINK   vs. Evans, 185

FINKELSTEIN   vs. Evans, 44

FLEISCHER   vs. Evans, 117

FLORES   vs. Evans, 132

FLORIDO   vs. Evans, 140

FRANK   vs. Evans, 58

GASSEN   vs. Evans, 175

GOLDWATER   vs. Evans, 46

GOLMAYO   vs. Steinitz, 6

GOMPERT   vs. Evans, 71

HALPER   vs. Evans, 70

HANAUER   vs. Evans, 86

HANS   vs. Evans, 161, 183

HARROLD   vs. Evans, 163

HARTLEB   vs. Evans, 139

HEARST   vs. Evans, 97, 120, 156, 160, 162

HEATH   vs. Evans, 119

HEINKENHEIMO   vs. Evans, 150

HESSE   vs. Evans, 172

HOWARD   vs. Evans, 31, 112

HOROWITZ   vs. Evans, 50

HUDSON   vs. Evans, 181

JACKSON   vs. Evans, 157

JACOBS   vs. Evans, 43

JIMENEZ   vs. Evans, 149

JOYNER   vs. Evans, 57

KAGETSU   vs. Evans, 116

KALME   vs. Evans, 74

KASHDAN   vs. Bisguier, 80; Evans, 22, 171

KATZ   vs. Evans, 83

KAUFMAN   vs. Evans, 61

KELLNER   vs. Evans, 159

KESTEN   vs. Evans, 59

KIESERITZKY   vs. Anderssen, 1

KÖNIG   vs. Evans, 106

KRAMER   vs. Bisguier, 9, 10; Evans, 95, 96, 142

KRAUSS   vs. Evans, 56, 147

LaBOURDONNAIS   vs. MacDonnell, 4

LAMBERT   vs. Evans, 167

LARSEN   vs. Evans, 23, 82, 177

LASKER   vs. Rubinstein, 187

LeCORNU   vs. Evans, 170

LEVIN   vs. Evans, 146

LOKVENCZ AND PRAVDA   vs. Evans and Spielberger, 125

LOMBARDY   vs. Evans, 194

LYMAN   vs. Evans, 88

MACCIONI   vs. Evans, 179

MACDONNELL	vs. LaBourdonnais, 4
MARRO	vs. Evans, 180
MAYER	vs. Evans, 143
McCORMICK	vs. Evans, 138, 145
MECHANIC	vs. Evans, 136
MEDNIS	vs. Evans, 182
MENGARINI	vs. Evans, 64
MORPHY	vs. Amateur, 5
NAJDORF	vs. Evans, 98
NASH	vs. Evans, 123
NIELSEN	vs. Evans, 124
NYHOLM	vs. Breyer, 15
OPSAHL	vs. Evans, 75, 76
PHILIDOR	vs. Smith, 3
PHILLIPS	vs. Evans, 122
PILNICK	vs. Evans, 154, 176
PLATER	vs. Evans, 153
POMAR	vs. Evans, 73
POSCHEL	vs. Evans, 40
QUESADA	vs. Evans, 126
REHBERG	vs. Evans,164
RESHEVSKY	vs. Evans, 174; D. Byrne, 42; Ståhlberg, 196
RÉTI	vs. Alekhine, 12, 13; Yates, 8
ROSS	vs. Evans, 45
ROSSOLIMO	vs. Evans, 14, 24
ROTHMAN	vs. Evans, 114
RUBINSTEIN	vs. Lasker, 187
SANDRIN	vs. Evans, 25, 151
SANTASIERE	vs. Evans, 90
SHAFFER	vs. Evans, 155
SHERWIN	vs. Bisguier, 84; Evans, 193
SMITH	vs. Philidor, 3
SMYSLOV	vs. Botvinnik, 53; Evans, 52
SPIELBERGER AND EVANS	vs. Lokvencz and Pravda, 125
STÅHLBERG	vs. Reshevsky, 196
STEINER	vs. Evans, 41, 87, 135, 144
STEINITZ	vs. Golmayo, 6
SUSSMAN	vs. Evans, 85
ULVESTAD	vs. Evans, 169
YATES	vs. Réti, 8